THE SEVEN
SPIRITUAL
SECRETS
OF SUCCESS

THE SEVEN SPIRITUAL SECRETS OF SUCCESS

RICHARD GAYLORD BRILEY

Publishers Since 1798

THOMAS NELSON PUBLISHERS

Nashville • Atlanta • London • Vancouver

Published in Nashville, Tennessee, by Thomas Nelson, Inc., Publishers, and distributed in Canada by Word Communications, Ltd., Richmond, British Columbia, and in the United Kingdom
by Word (UK), Ltd., Milton Keynes, England.

Scripture quotations are from the *Good News Bible*, Old Testament © 1976 by the American Bible Society; New Testament © 1966, 1971, 1976 American Bible Society. Used by permission.

Scripture quotations noted NKJV are from the NEW KING JAMES VERSION of the Bible.
Copyright © 1979, 1980, 1982, Thomas Nelson, Inc., Publishers.

Scripture quotations noted KJV are from The Holy Bible, KING JAMES VERSION.

Library of Congress Cataloging-in-Publication Data

Briley, Richard Gaylord, 1930—
      Seven spiritual secrets of success / Richard Gaylord Briley.
            p.   cm.
      ISBN 0-7852-8083-9
      1. Success—Religious aspects—Christianity. 2. Success—Biblical teaching. I. Title. II. Title;
7 Spiritual secrets of success.
BV4598.3.B75   1995
248.4—dc20   94-31738
                                                                                                          CIP

Printed in the United States of America

1 2 3 4 5 6 7 - 01 00 99 98 97 96 95

$\mathcal{D}$edicated to

Dr. Jim Taylor,
President of Cumberland College,
Williamsburg, Kentucky,
and his wife Dinah.

*The success they seek
is success for others.*

CONTENTS

THE SEVEN SPIRITUAL SECRETS

SECRET ONE

SECRET TWO

SECRET THREE

SECRET FOUR

SECRET FIVE

SECRET SIX

APPLYING THESE SECRETS
IN THE REAL WORLD

Does God Want *YOU* To Be a Success?

*I*n the Bible, when God needs something done, He always gives it to ONE PERSON to do—a Moses, a Peter, a Paul, a David, a Gideon, a Mary. Have you noticed?

One person, committed to a goal, is all God needs to change the world. He's done it many times. And if history turns many more pages, He will doubtless do it again.

This, then, is a book about one person—YOU—and the success-plans God has for those who believe and act on the message of the Bible. You and God together can change your world.

To get the most from this book, to find daring faith to act upon your God-given potential for success, you must already believe three things—

- That the Bible is *more* than humanity's oldest book of living wisdom—though it is at least that.
- That life has meaning.
- That your own life has a special purpose, even if that purpose and a plan to achieve it are not yet clear to you.

Success is a consequence, not an accident. It is the consequence of our timely actions and timeless beliefs. Long before science premised that all actions have reactions (consequences), the Bible promised the same.

We live, however, in a strange generation with confused goals, for it does not believe its acts have consequences. It takes risks, but has few goals worthy of them, unlike three hundred years of American families who risked in hope of self-betterment and helping their children to prosper.

As our first TV-reared generation (reflecting more input from advertisers than parents), it likes its problems solved by products, not by changes in behavior. It donates feverishly to find cures for diseases it will do little to avoid.

Denying its actions cause reactions, it has lost control of its future and demands, in compensation, that society be "fair"—that it gets what it wants, whether worked for and deserved, or not. This is sad for them, but good news for you.

It means 95 percent of the people you meet will never compete with you for success. Most don't know they are allowed to try. They lack what any goal-setting, successful 5 percent starts with—"permission" to try and to succeed.

The Soviet state, by killing off its successful 5 percent assured its own slow death and seventy-five years of poverty for its people, who were taught to believe success is a crime.

Unless you're a leftover Marxist, you don't feel that way, I'm sure. But what were you taught? Poverty is better? Success is a sin? It ruins the environment? It's bad for you? It's greedy? It angers God because it's so selfish?

Success is not selfish in its end result. In reaching our life goals, we do God's work, because our success creates more abundance for everyone to share! *This spillover is God's purpose behind all success in our work.*

Producing payoffs far off-the-scale for the work involved, creating a cushion of abundance that protects the human family from inevitable hard times—*that* is what success is all about. You don't have to take my word for it. If you read the Bible, you'll have God's Word for it.

Does God want you to be a success? The answer is in this question: Do YOU want you to be a success?

Richard Gaylord Briley
The Lady Blanche House
N.H. Historical Home (1970)
North Conway, New Hampshire

The Three-Way Test
for Success Goals

A True GOAL is an Objective that is
Life-enhancing, Specific, Measurable

True GOALS differ from dreams and hopes in their numeric quality, being concerned with achievement of things measured by quantity, size, quality, and time. **"What gets measured, gets done."**

Measurable · Specific · Life-enhancing

Wishes, hopes, and dreams may underlie a GOAL but will lack its specificity of purpose, of benefit, of timing, or any full awareness of an outcome's effect on others.

GOALS are meant to make life overall richer, fuller, happier, more enjoyable, longer, and better for many. The persons and creatures of God affected must not be exploited to their detriment.

$\mathcal{T}$he God Who Loves Success

*Remember that it is the LORD your God
who gives you the power to become rich . . .*
Deuteronomy 8:18

$\mathcal{G}$od wrote the book on success. We call it the Bible.

God is not in the failure business. The oldest story in the Bible is a success story! Few today know this since so few treat the Bible as our parents did, as God's guidebook for daily living. It tells us how to live, not just how to die, shows how to prosper, not just how to survive poverty.

Most scholars say the oldest book in the Bible is Job. It's more than a hard-luck tale. It tells of a good, successful man who loses everything on earth in a series of catastrophes. Later, he gets it all back, double for his trouble, at God's hand. God here shows us it's okay to succeed.

People often think God likes them *poor* and humble. But as Job's story and others in the Bible will show, He likes them just as well *rich* and humble.

Whatever God's reasons, Job's tale is an odd way to start off writing a holy book, if you think about it.

Pretend for a moment, you're God. You want someone to get down to the business of writing the first of the sixty-six books that will someday form our familiar Bible. Where do you have them start? Logic says *"In the beginning"*—with the book of Genesis—as the Bible does today.

Sounds like a good beginning to me: Cosmic forces crackling, the morning stars shouting together for joy, the drama of creation unfolding. Those who sifted the Bible into its presently accepted order thought so too. Genesis is where they start the Bible. Job's success story they plunk eighteen books toward the middle, next to the Psalms, as the first of the so-called poetical books.

But not God. He skipped Genesis and the Big Bang to start his first love letter to the human race by dealing with the problems of a rich and successful man! Not what you'd expect. Nothing much about the poor and hungry. Is it possible God never intended for mankind to live poor and hungry?

Whatever else God is, in getting the Bible written, He is down-to-earth. For the Bible's first-scripted book He chose something not of galactic scale, but an inspired human-sized tale suitable for a Western movie. It has cattle rustling, rampaging tribes, pestilence, firestorms, and a "great wind" that collapses the house of the eldest son, killing all Job's children. All this accomplished before the audience can get comfortably seated.[1]

The focus of all this wealth and violence is a well-off, upright individual God loves for His own reasons—Job the successful man of business. So successful is Job, his heirs do not have to work, his investments prosper, his livestock multiply, his abundance is legend, and his children are decent people who love their parents.

To this point in the story, God has prospered Job, protecting his wealth and health until the day He agrees to let Job be tested a little, to see if he still loves and obeys God if stripped of the trappings of success.

In testing Job, God is responding to bad talk about His servant, the jealous talk that often haunts the notably successful, inspiring doubts about them.

After the breathtaking action of the first two chapters, the rest of Job's story is quieter. It's mostly a campfire dialog between Job, now suffering with boils over all his body, and some not-too-helpful friends and his ready-to-give-up wife. They try to convince Job that his disastrous downfall is God's public payback for secret sins, connected somehow to Job's imagined misdeeds in quest of success.

With her children dead, her husband financially ruined and made untouchable by his oozing sores, Job's wife helpfully suggests suicide: *"Curse God and die."* Nobody rebukes her for this bad attitude, but later in the book she sides again with life and a hope-filled future by having more children.

In the final reel God has the last word, silencing Job's accusers. He finds nothing to condemn in the man, beyond failure to believe fully in the greatness and power of God, who now chooses to reward him with twice the wealth he possessed before the time of testing.

Life after death—where the only success is God's favor—is foreshadowed by Job's second family. Ten new children are born, but since his first seven sons and three daughters are presumed by the writer to be alive with God, the new set of siblings gives Job a total of twenty—double, like everything else.

SUCCESS OR SUFFERING?

Many modern readers pick up from Job's story only his suffering and pain. They don't see the underlying success story, obsessing themselves with misery. Some see themselves in a starring role, unjust sufferers like Job. ("*Why me, Lord?*" they ask. To which the book of Job answers, "*Why not?*" After all, Job endured much, yet the text says he was a man God found no fault with.)[2]

Leaping to the familiar terrain of pain, they neglect the story's start and finish, elements which lend this firstborn book of the Bible its unique sense and meaning. Namely, that God says, yes, a lot of suffering goes on in this world, but it's okay to succeed in your work if you can. The two subjects are not necessarily related.

We should never pick up the idea that Job's sufferings earned him his later success. God made Job work for every shekel of it: He blessed his hard work. God's blessing assured success, not Job's previous pain.

WORKING FOR SUCCESS

In ascribing credit to God for the abundance Job enjoyed, as the Bible does, let us remember that *Job worked for what he got*. Angels did not tend his flocks for him or balance his parchment ledgers. Nor did his business magically grow back overnight. He invested years of effort, time, and skill in rebuilding. God gave the increase, as it says elsewhere in the Bible,[3] but Job put in the work.

This shows in the last paragraphs of Job's story. After being told "the Lord gave Job twice as much as he had before," we are told this odd thing happened:

> *Then there came unto him all his brethren,*
> *and all his sisters, and all they*
> *that had been of his acquaintance before,*
> *and did eat bread with him in his house:*
> *and they bemoaned him, and comforted him*
> *over all the evil*
> *that the Lord had brought upon him:*
> *every man also gave him a piece of money,*
> *and every one an earring of gold.*
> (Job 42:11, KJV)

The Bible says it clearly; his friends and relatives gave him a grubstake to go back in business. They handed him enough capital to start again in a modest way: minted coins to deal with townspeople, pure gold to trade with strangers. It is not possible his friends gave him outright all that he accumulated before he died, for the Scripture's final ledger reads—

14,000 sheep
6,000 camels
1,000 oxen
1,000 donkeys.[4]

In today's market values these animals might be worth between $30 million and $50 million if sold for top dollar in the right marketplace. Job's fortune, even now, would command respect.

Accepting his friends' gifts as seed money, trading wisely, and breeding animals with care, Job rebuilt his flocks and his fortune, setting an example for entrepreneurs ever since, who often find they must succeed twice or more to make it stick.

ANOTHER USE FOR PATIENCE

If asked what virtue Job displayed, everyone would say "patience." Job's very name is a byword for tooth-gritting endurance. But were you to track his underlying success tale instead of the trail of tears, Job's patience shows up in a different light.

We're taught to think of his patience as helping him outlast a painful plight. But there is much more. For patience underlies success as well, that is, patience in the sense of persistence, repeated effort in the face of repeated failure. Patience is as much the pattern of the entrepreneur or success-seeker as of any biblical saint seeking to outlast painful hard times.

Job's patience helped his investments succeed.

Over time his patience increased his herds and flocks, earning riches on all his investments. Consider what business Job was in. It's not enough to read that he had so many sheep, camels, oxen, and donkeys. At some point *he had to do something with them*—eat them, sell them, turn their hides into something. He was not running a petting zoo.

It's reasonable, given hints in Scripture, that Job ran something like a used camel lot. Except for the sheep, the other animals, all 8,000 of them, were valuable in the transport and hauling business, in trade caravans. Job's business probably bestrode an important caravan junction. In this strong commercial environment, opportunities for investment and profit were above average.

God rewarded Job with an entrepreneur's most valuable gift—time! He was given extra years to exercise his well-practiced patience, but as an investor-businessman and not as a mournful sufferer or object of pity.

His time of sorrow taxed his patience a few weeks or a few months. After his restoration, Job lived 140 more years, two bonus biblical lifespans. For what purpose? To add further to his success!

A less hardy soul might have squandered God's gift years on self-pity, fearing to act boldly ever again, no matter how long life went on. Job used his bonus to increase the profit on his investments—and of God's investment in him.

In Job's story, the oldest piece of the Bible, God shows Himself the friend, investor, and champion of a persistent person who maximizes his God-given gifts to earn success in two realms—at work and at home.

God clearly is not against success. He took the trouble to let us see how one God-fearing man survived loss and failure and earned his success all over again. Then He took the tale and built the Holy Bible around it.

Success Summary

+ The Bible is the world's oldest "success book."
+ God pays attention to how we earn and share our successes.
+ Suffering is part of our human lot, but not our whole reason for being. The same is true of success.
+ Job's success came from his own efforts, with God's blessing.
+ God doesn't rejoice if you fail. He will help you try again if you want to succeed.

Scripture references
[1] Job 1:13-22
[2] Job 1:8
[3] 1 Corinthians 3:7
[4] Job 42:12–17

THE SEVEN
SPIRITUAL
SECRETS

$\mathcal{T}$he truest
meaning of
Success
is not
"To get
up on top"
but
"To get
out from under!"

SECRET
ONE

Success Bows to God's Purposes

And he shall be like a tree planted
by the rivers of water,
that bringeth forth his fruit in his season;
his leaf also shall not wither;
and whatsoever he doeth shall prosper.
Psalms 1:3, KJV

*I*n a universe that often seems on automatic pilot, God is in fact an active player.

He can use the physical things and events of our world to achieve His purposes. He distills purpose out of chaos.

We may think chaos the enemy of God's purposefulness. The fact is, all matter is structured on a platform of "perfect" chaos. Were the perfectly random movement of subatomic particles in any way predictable (and therefore "patterned"), the universe we know could not exist. It would self-destruct, fissured by those patterns. Chaos underlies its existence.

Before we get twenty words into the Bible, we find God organizing chaos to do His bidding. "The earth was without form, and void"[1] is how the Bible expresses this chaotic condition. But by the end of this second verse of Genesis, we see the spirit of God moving upon the face of the planet, bringing light and life to it.

In a world that to us seems chaotic and confused, God can work through seemingly random events to achieve His goals. For example:

- A stray current deposits the infant Moses at the feet of a princess bathing in the waters of the Nile. She becomes his foster mother.
- A fish drawn into a Galilean boat holds in its mouth the exact coin needed to pay a troublesome tax for Jesus' disciples.
- The unexpected passing of a band of traders bound for Egypt causes Joseph's jealous brothers to pull him from the dry well where they put him to die and sell him into slavery instead. By so doing they save his life and, years later, that of their entire family in time of famine.
- A North African strides into Jerusalem from the countryside, gets caught up in a passing crowd, and finds himself ordered by a Roman soldier to carry the cross of a criminal who has stumbled on the way to His execution. In time this black man becomes one of the first Christians and takes the Gospel story back to his own people.

What some may call a chance event is merely God doing something He's intended for a long time.

WHY SOME FAIL

God can use anything to achieve His purposes—even our failures. So why not our successes?

Many pray the Lord to redeem their failures and make something worthy of what's left, which is a way of asking for a miracle.

But fewer ask God to make something worthy of their best efforts and hoped-for success in the first place, which is strange. Success is not really miracle territory. Miracles result from the suspension of natural laws. Success results from following natural laws which the Bible teaches us. Prayer for success acknowledges this.

Failure often is the result of ignoring God. He does not like to be ignored.

James, believed to be the brother of Jesus, makes a point of this in his fiery little book in the New Testament. Speaking of businessmen who express an intention to go abroad for a year of trading and making money, he berates them for not including God in their plans for success. It is not that they intend to do wrong. They have just neglected to acknowledge God and His purposes in their plans.

James tells them to add a certain conditionality to their planning —

> *"Instead you ought to say this:*
> *'If the Lord wills,*
> *we will live and do this or that.'"*
> James 4:15

God does not need to be reminded that He is in charge by our uttering "Lord willing" at the end of every sentence. God is not dull. James's purpose is to keep us aware that God is at work in this world, "willing" the ends toward which history is moving. If He wants to tap us for some small job *en route* to our goal, we need to be flexible enough to slow down and cooperate. Even if we are not sure what is going on, we must be "willing" to go along.

We may look back years later and see that the great ventures that stirred our blood and took our time and energy achieved little that we hoped for. While other things, done in passing, with people God threw in our path, have prospered, though not always with ourselves as prime beneficiaries.

We are not always the focus of our own work and God intends it that way. When God is at work in our lives, we do better than we know.

THE TOWER OF BABEL

God does not like being left out of His people's plans. He created us for companionship and likes to be involved in our lives. Whatever the deeper meanings of the Tower of Babel story, [2] telling how mankind got scattered widely upon the face of the Earth, it is evident that heaven was not pleased with the God-excluding attitude of that generation.

Several generations had passed since Noah built an altar to the Lord after safely coming through the flood with his family and menagerie intact to replenish the Earth. In all that time we hear of no other structure being erected to honor God for His goodness or to thank Him for His blessings, not so much as a fencepost.

Now, a united people decide to put up a city and the world's tallest building to make a name for themselves. They fear being scattered away from the comfort of like-minded persons who have no use for God, only human achievement.

God is not mentioned, included, or invited.

Since God had given Noah a contract—one we still operate under, by the way—committing Himself to send no more universal floods and to provide regular "seedtime and harvest" till the end of the world, the people owed Him at least a grunt of acknowledgment, if not thanks. But they would give nothing.

Not only did they want to ignore God, they strongly distrusted Him. This is portrayed by the materials they used, the site they chose, and the fact that they built the tower. God promised through Noah never again to flood the earth, but this generation did not believe Him.

The clues are three:

1) They built on a dry plain where rainfall was so infrequent irrigation was the only assured way to grow crops.
2) They built the world's tallest tower for refuge in case of another flood.
3) They built with waterproof materials, using fire-hardened brick,

which cannot melt away in rain or flood like sun-dried brick, and used petroleum tar for mortar, which cannot leach away in water.

Their attitude toward God was grudge, not gratitude. So He disrupted their ability to communicate with each other and they left off building the city since they could no longer work together. Success would forever elude them.

As God disrupted their plan, He observed that even this early in human history, if people were of one mind and one language "nothing will be restrained from them, which they have imagined to do."[3] In other words, people working together can build almost any kind of world they want, even a godless one.

But the first time anyone tried, God stopped them. Others would try later, but by then God had Himself a chosen people under contract to be His witnesses and beneficiaries in each generation.

If there are lessons for us in the Babel story, one is that either God enters into the goals we plan or we cannot expect His help in reaching them—and may even anticipate His opposition. Another is that people who, like the tower builders, constantly expect evil to rain down from God (even in the mild form of "bad luck") cannot reasonably hope for success. They do not *fear* God—hold Him in reverential awe—they are *afraid* of Him.

NO SECRET RULES FOR SUCCESS

The rules of success are not secret. We find them in the Bible and other places. Even by the earliest torchlight of prehistory, we see some already being shared in symbolic pictures painted on the walls of caves. Later, as civilization (city-living) dawned, "wisdom book" collections of rules and sayings about successful living (or dying—*The Book of the Dead*, for example) were perennial "bestsellers."

The great underground galleries of prehistoric animal art in Spain, France, and elsewhere were not mere rainy-day diversions for those who drew and painted them over the many centuries they accumulated. Created with a force that stirs us even today, their apparent intent was to help older men teach young boys the rules of successful manhood, young men the spiritual rules of successful hunting.

Books of "wisdom sayings," sounding like a Middle Eastern *Poor Richard's Almanac*, were inscribed in clay and painted on papyrus before the Egyptians completed their pyramids or the Mesopotamians their canal-lined cities. Many of the success principles we follow were already identified and being used to energize great enterprises, as they do today.

The use of these simple idea-tools lets a small handful of motivated people shape the world, for good or ill, in each generation. These tool concepts are commonplace to Western culture and expressed with insight in the Bible.

But like any wisdom too well said or too well known, the rules of success are frequently esteemed too simple to be effective, too trite to be true. This, despite fossil imprints of them found in both Testaments of the Bible, attesting to their early discovery and long use by those who fathered prosperity.

THE BIBLE SAYS IT BETTER

Where we say "success" the Bible says "prosper." In many ways prosper is the better word. Pull it apart and the word *prosper* (Latin *pro*=for; *sper*=hope) reveals its original meaning—"according to (your) hopes."

"To prosper" means to get what you hope for. (Not a bad definition of success!) We need high hopes, for what we hope for, we surely pray for and work for as well.

The ancient path to success or "getting what you hope for," as we shall trace it in other parts of this book, is simply this:

1) Set a measurable goal.
2) Hold a clear vision of that goal.
3) Form a plan to reach the goal.
4) Follow your plan to reach the goal.

It is mostly at the last point—execution of your master plan—that the ancient rules for success and right living show up. Everything to this point is mere mental exercise, not a molecule of matter being moved. Here we start bumping into people, and there's the rub. They have rights too; as many as we. Whatever we do to get "what we hope for," must not hurt others. Like physicians' oath of Hippocrates, the primary Law of Success is "First, do no harm."

Those who don't mind injuring others for personal gain sometimes excuse it by saying, "You can't make omelettes without breaking eggs." They play a cruel shell game, for success is no omelette. It can be gained without harming others or injuring their rights. The Bible demands no less.

SOCK THE RICH

Somewhere after Job and Genesis, the Bible starts to crack down on the rich. Up to this point, most of its main characters own or control large wealth—Job, Abraham, Isaac, Jacob, Joseph, Moses. Adam owned everything. By the time of the prophets, a rich-man-as-villain trend is well defined in Bible thought. The rich are routinely warned and spoken against. God seems to quit dealing with rich elders like Job and start working with poor youths like David. What caused this shift?

What changed were the means and the measure of wealth, centuries after the biblical patriarchs departed. It was no longer a cattle culture. Wealth could now be piled up by exploiting creatures with two legs, not four.

Riches were no longer measured in herds or "the wealth of blood" as nomads even today call their investment in livestock. The first successful persons in Scripture were self-employed herders, followed by administrators like Joseph, Moses, and Daniel, who worked for wealthy governments. After the patriarchs, the system no longer depended on herdsmen or lived off their alms. Society began basing itself on small farmers, self-sufficient and mostly poor, but with some surplus to sell townsmen.

Were Abraham's heirs, the Israelites, to gain their promised numbers, they must till and fill the land flocks once grazed. The growth of villages and towns, supported by farmers in the surrounding countryside, led to more complicated commerce, calling for lenders, lawyers, clerks, and enforcers. It was not far different from the settling of the American West in the 1800s.

The Bible's chief grievance against the wealthy lay not in their money, but in how they made their money.

Scripture calls for equity and fair play. Blatant abuse of the legal system by the rich, taking the poor to court and depriving them of their living, was, by the days of the prophets, impoverishing the helpless. The well-off perverted a system meant to provide justice for all and denied it to orphans, widows, and the working poor.

At this point and for this reason, the Bible turns on the rich. James echoes the same thoughts centuries later in a virtual tirade against the wealthy.[4] His anger is leveled at them for not paying their workers and for condemning the innocent to poverty and, indirectly, death. Their luxury appalls him for it is based on the blood of the poor.

Out of Bible texts like these grew an anti-wealth philosophy that has swayed many over the centuries. For its sake people even today deny themselves (and others) the right to pursue success—for fear success might lead to the creation of forbidden wealth. One can look at the failed Communist systems and see their anti-wealth motivation in the same half-reading of Scripture. (Communism, as others have amply pointed out, was a kind of heretical Christianity.)

But the Bible does not forbid wealth. It only forbids the misuse of others in the pursuit of it. And it denounces the misuse of accumulated wealth, for which it recommends the expiation of showing mercy to the poor.[5]

While God may choose not to create everyone equal in talent, size, strength, and brainpower, He insists that we treat each other fairly. Otherwise we are unjust and whatever we gain as a result is ill-gotten, our seeming success doomed.

> *"Better is a little righteousness*
> *than great revenues without right."*
> Proverbs 16:8, KJV

This demand for fairness extends, in the Bible, to a call for "just balances, just weights" [6] (honesty, in a word) in all business transactions. And, in the book of James, comes a demand that we treat other people as God sees them, not as a credit bureau might classify them.

If we mean to prosper, to get what we hope for—to succeed—the

Bible shows we must start by respecting the rights of others before we take for ourselves.

Since the successful few achieve much of what any society does, they have an impact that outweighs their relatively small number. They set the tone for everyone. By bowing to God's purposes in their success, they help assure prosperity for themselves and help the angels accomplish God's will on Earth as it is in heaven.

SUCCESS SUMMARY

+ Success is not a miracle; it follows natural laws.
+ "Chance events" can be God at work in our lives.
+ Failure is often the result of ignoring God or not trusting Him.
+ Biblical "prosperity" (success) means getting what you hope for and, therefore, pray for.
+ Success achieved at the cost of injuring others is tainted.
+ The Bible does not forbid wealth, only the misuse of its power and the misuse of others in acqiring it.

If we truly pray for God's will to be done on Earth, we don't have to search out every detail of His purpose in our lives before finding success. It is only when we seek or use our success selfishly

16

*that we can't count on Heaven's help. Check out
Deuteronomy 8:11 and James 4:3.*

Scripture references

[1] Genesis 1:2 (NKJV)

[2] Genesis 11:1-9

[3] Genesis 11:6 (KJV)

[4] James 5:1-6

[5] Daniel 4:27

[6] Leviticus 19:36 (KJV)

SECRET
TWO

Success Calls for a Successor

. . . Obey everything written in it. Then you will be
prosperous and successful.
Joshua 1:8

$\mathcal{T}$he God of the Bible is a deal-making, contract-writing, contract-honoring God.

At different times in history, He sought out certain persons and offered them a contract to be their God if they would be His people. Any deal we have with Him today comes through them; we bought into their contract.

Abraham was one of the first with a contract. Jacob another. And David. With each He made a conditional contract (a covenant or testament) couching His offer in lawyerly language: "If you will do so and so, I will do such and such."

Today we divide the Bible into an Old Testament and a New Testament to reflect the differences in these contracts God made, at various times, with those who would be His people and our spiritual ancestors.

At Sinai, where Moses came down the mountain with God's Law in hand, a whole nation, the tribes of Israel, freshly fled from Egyptian slavery, voiced its pledge to accept God's contract. It was an offer they could not refuse.

For without this contract for God's help, they were merely another wandering Semitic tribe with no fixed abode and no assured existence. With the covenant, they were assured of a *Land* and a *Law*—a place to live and a way to live. God would do His promised part if they did theirs. Then they would enjoy "good success."

To our Bible's English translators, working only a few years before the Pilgrims landed at Plymouth Rock, *success* meant simply "outcome." They spoke of "*good* success" because it was still possible to speak of "*bad* success," i.e., bad consequences. *Success* had yet to take on its restricted modern meaning *as a good consequence only*.

So, the verse means if the Israelites upheld their part of God's bargain, consequences would be good. This helps us remember that success is a consequence, a consequence of actions taken, and not an accidental outcome.

This verse in Joshua is the only place in the entire Bible that our word *success* appears at all in the traditional King James translation.

This does not mean that the concept of success, as we speak of it, is unknown in the Bible. To the contrary, as we shall see, the Bible is remarkable in its perceptions about success, but starts at a vastly different viewpoint: God's.

Success Requires a Successor

Consider the problem an Eternal Being faces in trying to draw up an enforceable contract with a mortal being that's mostly water and is so short-lived it feels fortunate to see one thousand full moons in a lifetime.[1] God will exist forever to uphold His end of the agreement; we mortals rejoice to exceed a biblical lifespan of threescore and ten. What good is a long-term contract with God if you can't live long enough to collect on it?

In the Bible we find two creative solutions:

1) God grants His people eternal life so He and they can enjoy each other's company and the benefits of their covenant forever.
2) In the Bible there is never a success without a successor to continue the contract.

The first solution is simple and satisfying. Death is not allowed to end life for God's people; it becomes like a beaded curtain dividing two living areas from each other. It resolves the problem out of the earthly sphere to a heavenly sphere.

It also does something else. For the first time, *it gives humans a rationale for heaven*; explains why God should invent it in the first place. Heaven—as someplace more than God's private abode or business address, as a place filled with what Jesus called "dwelling places"[2] for His saints—exists so God can fulfill the terms of His agreements with

23

us mortals. It's a place prepared for beings granted the gift of eternal life, so they can live out their contract with God—forever. On the day of creation, it did not exist. Jesus said it was a place He was going away to prepare.

In effect, like a family that adds a wing to its house so other members can move in, God has put a new subdivision in Heaven to house those who love Him. God was not duty-bound to move over, as it were, and make room for us. That He did is due to His promises. He goes to great lengths to keep them.

The second solution is more subtle. It is God's apparent way of dealing with the problem of human brevity in and on the physical plane of Earth. There is never a success, in Scripture, without provision for a successor, someone to carry on the work, someone to receive the benefits of the covenant, the continuing contract with God.

Physical death of the frailer party does not void the deal. It continues in full force, from generation to generation. The success of God's purpose is assured by the presence of a legal successor to the original contract, just as in our law, in which a contract is binding upon "heirs, successors, and assigns."

Do we need to look for proof?

We can start with father Abraham, the friend of God, the great pattern believer. The contract God gave to Abraham is never mentioned without reference to Abraham's descendants, his "seed," his successors.

24

For all the land which thou seest, to thee
will I give it, and to thy seed for ever.
Genesis 13:15, KJV

God goes to some effort to see that Abraham, hovering near ninety-nine at the time, gets a biological heir, which he's never had. God's real estate contract with Abraham must lapse if there are no assured successors for the old man. Years later, when son Isaac needs a wife, the Bible describes in rich, poetic detail the quest for one, to show future claimants that Abraham's bloodline (and land claim) indeed continue.

This demand for physical continuity adds drama and excitement to places in Scripture where it seems God's promise may be jeopardized. As when Abraham, in obedient faith, prepares to sacrifice his only son, knowing this death would ruin everything. And when baby Moses is cast adrift in a bulrush basket to escape the mass killing of Hebrew infants—and is rescued to be raised by Pharaoh's daughter and lead his people from bondage in Egypt.

The slaughter of babies and toddlers in Judea near the time of Christ's birth, by Herod the Roman puppet, was another attempt to destroy God's promised genetic line to Abraham's ultimate Successor, the Messiah.

Jesus Christ is, of course, that Ultimate Successor, and He successfully saw to His end of the contract, our atonement by His death and resurrection. But even He left a successor—the Holy Spirit.

As Jesus neared His crucifixion, the gathered disciples heard Him say:

> *I will pray the Father, and he shall give you another*
> *Comforter, that he may abide with you for ever,*
> *even the Spirit of truth.*
> John 14:16–17

> *. . . If I go not away, the Comforter will not come*
> *unto you; but if I depart, I will send him unto you.*
> John 16:7

In the most literal sense, the church, indwelt by the Holy Spirit, is the successor to Christ on Earth, serving in His place until He returns. The Church Triumphant, that is, the Church Successful, will hand its spiritual authority over to Christ at that time.

THE SUCCESSOR PRINCIPLE

There are many examples in Scripture of the Success/Successor Principle. We will deal with the principle's implications a little further on.

The dark centuries between the death of Joshua, who led the Israelites into the Land of Promise, and the rise of their first king were dangerous because no one succeeded Joshua in title, rank, or ability.

He had no successor, probably because he had only an incomplete success.

His assignment was to cross the River Jordan with his armies, possess the Land, and drive out or dominate its previous occupants, which he did not fully do. So it was hundreds of years before the Jewish tribes were strong enough to control the land and live in peace. They were led sporadically by an irregular series of "judges," like Samson, to battle with the Philistines.

The first Jewish king was Saul, and he did not succeed at the task either, and left no successor. He was displaced by David, who battled the enemy, united the country and, being successful at Joshua's assignment at last, left a succession of kings to rule the land, starting with Solomon.

A man could neither live nor die successfully without a successor. In Old Testament law, if a man's brother died childless, it was the duty of the survivor to have a child by the widow. As Scripture goes on to say, "It shall be that the firstborn which she beareth shall succeed in the name of [the] brother which is dead, that his name be not put out of Israel".[3]

The Jews of old had the duty of racial continuity (hence, an obligation to marry and raise a family), so Abraham would always have heirs for his contract with God.

God also made a covenant with David, the shepherd boy who killed Goliath with the giant's oversized sword after felling him with a slingshot. David is described in the Bible as a man after God's own heart.[4] Their contract provided that God would always provide an heir to David's throne. This He did in the eternal person of Jesus of Nazareth, who is a direct descendant of David.

Because of bloodguilt, David was forbidden the crowning act of his career, to erect a temple for the Lord. So he spent years assembling and stockpiling construction materials for his son and successor, who built the great Temple of Solomon.

David successfully united the land and staved off all enemies. Solomon successfully exploited the long peace that followed, giving ancient Israel its true golden age. They both succeeded, and God's succession continued.

WHAT THE SUCCESSION PRINCIPLE TELLS US

Success is often seen as a "winner-take-all" achievement, a solitary conquest meant to be savored alone by the victor, whose personal satisfaction is his only aim in life. The entertainment media makes this a frequent plot premise, presenting a "lone gunman" as hero or anti-hero who lives for the moment. The Succession Principle presents us with a different standard.

1) Success in the Bible takes the long view.
The Bible's idea of success always goes beyond the moment of success to involve continuity and a long view of life. Success does not stand isolated. It is a knot in the fabric of history that introduces a new thread into the future pattern.

Take David's one-boy victory over Goliath, for example. The story in the book of 1 Samuel presents no solitary, self-centered hero. He sees beyond the moment. When he picks up stones for his slingshot, he selects not one or two nor a half dozen. He chooses exactly "five smooth stones."[5]

In so choosing, he is already seeing beyond a personal victory against the Philistine champion. He knows the enemy has four oversized "giants of Gath" like Goliath[6] and victory may be brief if he's not ready to dispatch them as well. So he prepares to deal with them if he must. His success gives courage to the armies of the Lord. Even as he holds aloft the gory head of Goliath, they attack and the Philistines run. After four long centuries, Philistine mastery begins to crumble—because of one boy's success.

Success that focuses on succession—on what comes afterward—cannot help being more substantial and lasting in effect than that aimed at short-term gain. Not every goal we set must have one-hundred-year consequences, but we are better off selecting purposes with enduring payoffs.

2) Success in the Bible leaves something for tomorrow and for others.

David's personal success did not reduce other people's opportunities for success. His victory inspired many others that day to acts of courage that led to success for the armies of the fledgling kingdom of Israel.

Of the many models for success in the Bible, another is Boaz, "a mighty man of wealth" and great-grandfather of David.[7] He possessed bountiful fields outside of Bethlehem, the family hometown. In the touching love story that composes the little Bible book of Ruth, we come across Boaz watching his reapers at harvest, with gleaners following behind to pick up for themselves whatever the harvesters miss or drop. Among the gleaners is Ruth, the young widow he will eventually marry.

Jewish law allowed the poor to glean all fields, taking as their own whatever grain fell or was overlooked. The landowners were required by the law to allow this, to leave something for others. But Boaz did more.

He instructed his field hands, "Let her glean even among the sheaves . . . and let fall also some of the handfuls of purpose for her, and leave them, that she may glean them . . .".[8]

The truly successful never forestall the success of others, if they can help it, but leave something for others to do and something for the long tomorrow.

3)   Success in the Bible is not always achieved in one's own name.

The Bible does not teach that all success is to be sought for selfish or tightly personal reasons. Often the success God seeks to work through us does as much for others as for ourselves.

While the affection of Boaz for Ruth was real, he was, the Bible story clearly says, a "near kinsman" and thus obliged, if there were no one more closely related, to marry her and buy back any property Ruth's

30

dead husband left behind. As it happened, there was a closer kinsman, but he had an inheritance to protect, so signed off his obligation to Boaz on request.

In the town gate Boaz said, "Ruth the Moabitess, the wife of Mahlon, have I purchased to be my wife, to raise up the name of the dead upon his inheritance, that the name of the dead be not cut off from among his brethren . . .".[9]

When their son was born, "they called his name Obed: he is the father of Jesse, the father of David".[10]

In reaching his goal (one of the definitions of success) and marrying Ruth, Boaz had to forget himself first. He could succeed in wedding her only if he did so to perpetuate the name of his deceased kinsman, Mahlon. So he did. And this is the only reason Mahlon's name comes down to us to this very day. Or that of Boaz.

For while the law was served, and Obed's birth preserved the genetic continuity of dead Mahlon's line as closely as possible, God was kind. In fathering Obed—as Mahlon's surrogate—Boaz entered the gene line of Jesus.

Boaz found success and a successor only when he allowed himself to seek his success in the name of, and for the benefit of, another, the way Jesus later did.

SUCCESS SUMMARY

+ Success is a planned outcome, not an accident.
+ Success demands a successor—to live with its consequences.
+ Success takes the long view, not a short one.
+ Success leaves something for tomorrow and for others; it is not greedy.
+ Success may have to be achieved in the name of others, not just by "looking out for number one."

God's purpose in all success is to create new abundance to assure the survival of the human family—our successors—in bad times and good. In the long geneaologies in the Bible (with all those "begats") each person is another successor, whose ultimate successor was Jesus of Nazareth.

Footnotes and Scripture references

[1] At 13 full moons a year, about 77 years
[2] John 14:2
[3] Deuteronomy 25:6, KJV
[4] 1 Samuel 13:14 and Acts 13:22
[5] 1 Samuel 17:40
[6] 2 Samuel 21:22
[7] Ruth 2:1, KJV
[8] Ruth 2:15–16, KJV
[9] Ruth 4:10, KJV
[10] Ruth 4:17, KJV

*O*bedience
is the
minimum
God expects
of us.
Success
is the
maximum.

SECRET
THREE

Success Benefits Others First

*But others fell on good ground
and yielded a crop: some a
hundredfold, some sixty,
some thirty.*
Matthew 13:8

Success is a multiplier, not a divider. It makes more for everybody, doubling the wealth of humanity.

By multiplying the effect of our effort, success serves as God's way of benefitting others even while you seek to benefit yourself. Success is not as selfish as some would make it seem.

Success generates out-of-proportion payoffs. The seed of a good idea or a wise investment, as the Bible (and the stock market) show, can repay itself thirty, sixty, or one hundred times and more. These payoffs are what

1) make society run,
2) make jobs available,
3) make charity possible.

True success always spills over to benefit many beyond the few who took the risk of trial, error, and investment.

So long as the poor, the lame, and the blind dwell among us, we will need successful men and women among us too. We dare not eradicate them as a class or confiscate all their earnings to satisfy mistaken philosophies or political greed. For it is their surplus—the goods, money, jobs, and energy thrown off by the highly successful few—that provides extra portions for the needy and makes possible a decent society for all.

By individual success, society enriches itself. It makes its gains through us. Successful men and women are the roots that feed the tree of civilization. Eliminate us for whatever reason, and the tree dies a slow death.

(Ask the Russians about this. The Soviet state tried to disallow success for anyone, in the name of equality and fairness. The blunder took seventy years to catch up with them, but it did. Millions died for nothing.)

EQUAL OPPORTUNITY; UNEQUAL RESULTS

In creating life, God made a system where results are lopsided, biased in favor of more life. It takes only two fertile organisms and time to replace a million deaths. Life is fundamentally equal in opportunity and unequal in results. Jesus discussed this disproportion in the parable of a man sowing grain.

Most of the sower's effort is wasted. Half his grain is devoured or lost before it can sprout. What sprouts does not produce uniformly. Yet the planter gets a crop, and we can tell, by the numbers Jesus gave, that a minority of the seed produced the majority of the harvest. This is the rule of life. It is the law of success.

This universal Law of Disproportionate Rewards, when applied in my own profession (fund-raising), I speak of as the Five Percent Rule. In its general form it says:

> *Five percent of any voluntary group*
> *does 50% of whatever it is the group does.*[1]

Half of any firm's sales tend to get made by 5 percent of its sales force. Half the arrests by police usually involve the same 5 percent of the arrested population.

Business has long known that 20 percent of its efforts can generate 80% of its profits. But here is something tighter and more specific. I stumbled over this lopsided "5 percent makes 50 percent" payoff pattern in my years as a major fund-raising writer and strategist for large charities. I later found that this pattern, or something much like it, was there in the Bible all the time.

After I became privy to the statistics of many large fund-raising enterprises, a flash of insight concerning this unexpected 5 percent pattern hit me: Any charity beyond its infancy always gets half its income from a tiny 5 percent of its supporters, that is, one donor in twenty. One inspired donor gives as much as nineteen ordinary donors lumped together.

This knowledge conferred a distinct advantage on me and my clients, for it gave me a lever with which to multiply their income rapidly. And mine. All we had to do was identify our prolific five percent, and the rest was easy.

Years of study show the "5/50" pattern appears widely, suggesting it is common to most voluntary human activities, good and bad. (If many examples are negative, it has to do with why agencies collect statistics. Happiness is not statistical and good news rarely gets reported in the same proportion as bad.) Note the pattern we find—

- Half of any church's income usually comes from 5% of its supporters. Charities find the same.
- Five percent of convicted burglars commit half the break-ins. Repeat criminals do half our crimes.
- Half the beer in America is drunk by 5% of the beer drinkers.
- Half our people, in theory, are female, yet women constitute only 5% of the U.S. federal prison population.
- Five percent of car renters cause rental firms 50% of their major lawsuits.

Do arithmetic on Jesus' parable of the sower and similar imbalances appear:
- 25% of the seed birds eat

- 25% doesn't sprout
- 25% is choked out by weeds
- 25% produces a crop

Yet even the productive 25% varies in output:

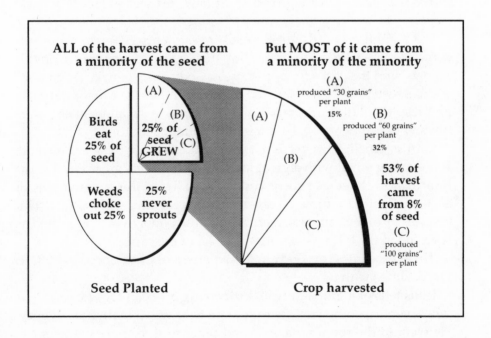

ALL of the harvest came from a minority of the seed

(A)
(B)
25% of seed GREW (C)

Birds eat 25% of seed

Weeds choke out 25%

25% never sprouts

Seed Planted

But MOST of it came from a minority of the minority

(A)
produced "30 grains" per plant
15%

(B)
produced "60 grains" per plant
32%

(A)

(B)

53% of harvest came from 8% of seed

(C)
produced "100 grains" per plant

(C)

Crop harvested

- 1/3 of the plants produce 30 grains each
- 1/3 produce 60 grains
- 1/3 produce 100 grains

The last third—about 8 percent of the total seed sown—gave 53% of the crop!

We inhabit a world where small investments generate large outcomes, where a little produces a lot. It is the pattern of nature on this planet—and the pattern of our success. God chose to make it that way. A small seed produces a giant redwood tree. A microscopic ovum splits and resplits until it becomes a mature whale. A small business starts out and becomes a global giant in the founder's lifetime.

Starting small, however, is not what makes life or a business succeed. It is starting small with a great idea. In nature this "great idea" is the information stored as genetic code in each living thing, patterning all aspects of life. In success-seekers, the "great idea" is the goal that inspires us to seek success, merged with the patterns of God's mind as revealed in the Bible. Goals are the DNA of the soul.

There is no question God applies a pattern of unbalanced payoffs in His dealings with us.

Jesus tells of a grape grower with an urgent need for workers.[2] His vines were ripening fast. Getting more help was a matter of urgency. He went to the town square several times to find more workers. He hired some at nine, noon, three, and five in the afternoon. To all he hired, whether taken on early or late, he gave the same pay: one piece of silver.

The point of Jesus' story was the reaction of the men hired early, who sweated and labored longest in the heat of the day for an agreed-to fair wage. It angered them that those hired late got the same pay they did, without working as long. But the owner said, as God does, "Don't I have the right to do what I wish with my own money? Or are you jealous because I am generous?"

GOD IS NOT FAIR

That's the problem with God. He is not fair. He is generous! In rewarding, He gives "good measure, pressed down, and shaken together, and running over."[3] In punishing, He gives only what we deserve.

Since the Bible insists none of us are born good, getting what we deserve could be severe punishment indeed. (If God gives more good than we deserve, that's grace. If He gives less evil than we deserve, that's mercy.)

It is this matter of fair punishment that figures in the Bible's story of Jonah. He was successful for God and for a large number of grateful people but not really happy about it. It irked him that God might not be stern enough in punishing the enemies of his people. He wanted no part of them.

Jonah, however, was a prophet of God. A prophet's job, when God called him to duty, was to take a specific message to a specific people at a specific time, usually "now." Today, when one can get a timely and timeless message from God by turning to the Bible, as we are this moment, God makes less use of prophets. But before the Bible was complete, they were necessary, as town criers were before newspapers.

Not all prophets were successful in their work of persuasion. None were popular, of course, for that goes with the trade. But Jonah, by the end of his four-chapter book, finds himself an unqualified success . . . and hating it. Petulantly, yet with good reason, he wanted to hate the very people God insisted he preach to.

They were Ninevites, bitter enemies of his own nation, living along the Tigris River in northern Iraq, near modern Mosul. Nineveh was a metropolis so big, the Bible says, it took three days to walk through. Jonah was told to get himself there and tell the people they had forty days before God destroyed them all.

Jonah had bad feelings about his assignment. He feared success. He suspected if he did as God said, the Ninevites might repent and so might God. That is, He could turn aside from His announced intention to punish them. (Close reading shows that when Jonah finally did proclaim God's message, there was no offer of mercy in it, only a declaration of impending punishment.)

Success did not interest Jonah. Nor did mingling with people he had been carefully taught to hate. So he headed in the opposite direction, toward a point nearly four times farther off by sea than Nineveh was by land. He booked last-minute passage on a merchant ship to Spain, out of the port of Joppa on the Mediterranean coast.

If the success of a prophet is measured by how many people believe his message and repent, then Jonah gets one of the highest success ratings in the Bible. Even while running from God, confessing to the captain and crew that the sudden storm endangering them all was his fault, his words inspired repentance. After the crew members, pagans all, reluctantly drop him overboard (at his insistence), the sea instantly stills. Stunned, they pledge themselves to worship the true and living God.

Later in Nineveh, Jonah marches silently a full day, a third of the way into the city, opens his mouth to preach only once, and the whole huge city repents in sackcloth and ashes. God evidently chose the right person for the job.

Jonah did his best to avoid facing God and his assignment. Yet he was a success at his work, despite himself.

There are times reported in the careers of the God-fearing, people marked by great success, when their deeds seem inevitable, preordained, unstoppable. Jonah's is such a case. God had no one better to send.

Jonah does the barest minimum of what God says to do—and it works. When God is behind a plan, it can succeed despite every human frailty and obstacle.

Jonah is, we must admit, an unusual case. His success, while his own and blessed by God, was not the result of some deep-seated drive of his own. It was God working out His purposes in His servant's life. Jonah's success most definitely was not for himself. It was for all the people his preaching saved from destruction.

Some people are more comfortable treating the Jonah story as a kind of child's tale, not worthy of serious attention by adults. But Jesus referred to Jonah as a historic character whose unusual adventures paralleled His own destiny.[4] We have to give the story of Jonah full weight.

SUCCESS WITHOUT GOD

In Jonah's case, miraculous events were involved in getting the prophet to a place where he could preach and witness the greatest success of his career. But as we saw earlier, success itself does not require miracles. If rain can fall on the just and the unjust alike, so can success befall the unworthy. Success is the fruit of natural laws, not supernatural interventions.

Nowhere in Scripture is this more clearly shown than in the parable Jesus told of a rich farmer. He is a man so successful his barns cannot hold all his crops. So he resolves to tear them down and build greater.

This farmer's success is built not on his superior brain power, marketing skill, or agricultural ability. His prosperity lies only in the fact that he owns very good farmland, some of the best. It is God's doing, not his. He probably inherited the land, so perhaps even its acquisition was not a matter to his credit.

- His success lay in being the owner of a productive piece of ground.
- His failure lay in keeping the fruits of his success for himself alone.

With self-satisfaction he faced the prospect of another bumper crop saying, "I have nowhere to bestow my goods." It was as good as saying there were no hungry people in the land on whom to bestow his surplus, there were no orphans or widows without a protector who could use food that winter, there were no empty barns or cupboards of the poor that needed filling.

Had he planned to build bigger barns to warehouse more food to do some good for others, he might have survived. But he doesn't make it through the night. God intervenes when He hears the farmer's self-congratulatory self-talk. What the man says is like the prayer of a self-made man worshiping his creator:

I will say to myself, "Lucky man!
You have all the good things you need for many years.
Take life easy, eat, drink, and enjoy yourself!"
But God said to him, "You fool!
This very night you will have to give up your life;
then who will get all these things
you have kept for yourself?"
Luke 12:19–20

47

Jesus added a footnote, "This is how it is with those who pile up riches for themselves but are not rich in God's sight."[5] There is an accountability that goes with the wealth production unleashed by success.

Not all the biblical rich had this problem. Joseph, a rich man from the town of Arimathea, was a follower of Jesus, said in Mark's gospel to be "an honorable counselor."[6] It was he who went to Pilate after the execution of Jesus to ask for the body to place in his own newly-hewn rock grave.

Consider too the wealth of Luke, the Greek physician who was St. Paul's sometime traveling companion, the author of a Gospel and the book of Acts. He had to be fairly well-off, as good physicians tend to be. His resources he put at the disposal of the early church as its first press agent and reporter.

He had money for travel and research. In the first few verses of his account of the life of Christ, Luke says, "I have carefully studied all these matters from their beginning . . . to write an orderly account for you."[7] Details he gives concerning the birth of Jesus and what went on in Mary's mind at the time show Luke sought her out to get her personal story. He inquired of others then living, who had known Jesus in the flesh. Only someone of means could afford the leisure and costs of travel to conduct this kind of research.

THE LOVE FOR RICHES

In dealing with Scripture and finding analogies other than those explicitly given by the writers or explained elsewhere in the book, we have to avoid conclusions that contradict the clear message of the Bible.

Jesus told the rich farmer parable to illustrate the impending kingdom of God, which His own people were shortly to reject, postponing most of its promises to a time yet future to us. He spoke against—not the rich but—those who love riches. There is a difference.

Read the whole text and you see that He said not to be obsessed with riches or worry. Both of them choke out God's message and keep it from growing in us. In my own experience as fund-raiser for many worthy causes, raising over time some two billion dollars, the people I found obsessed with riches were rarely the rich, but mostly the poor. Perhaps not the literal poor, but the unmonied. They had a ruthless belief, some of them, that money could supply all their needs. They lack experience with money.

Jesus said not to be obsessed with collecting riches, but not to be obsessed with collecting trivia either, in the form of worries about this life. Jesus said neither of these should stand in the way of our bearing fruit for God.

We must keep in mind that success does not always mean the pursuit of riches. It means the attainment of goals that are consistent with God's love for us. One of these goals, in our seeking for God-blessed success, is that it should always help and bless others.

Success Summary

+ Success is God's way of blessing others while you benefit yourself.
+ FIve percent of any voluntary group does fifty percent of whatever it is the group does.
+ God is not fair; He is generous.
+ Riches are far from being the only purpose for success.
+ Success may have to be achieved in the name of others, not just by "looking out for number one."

The most dangerous person is the "self-made man" who worships **his** *creator and looks out only for Number One.*

Footnotes and Scripture references
[1] *Are You Positive*, R. G. Briley, 1988 Berkley Publishing Group
[2] Matthew 20:1–16
[3] Luke 6:38, KJV
[4] Matthew 12:39–40
[5] Luke 12:21
[6] Mark 15:43, KJV
[7] Luke 1:3

SECRET
FOUR

$\mathcal{S}$uccess Starts with Permission

. . . To them gave he power
to become the sons of God.
John 1:12, KJV

$\mathcal{A}$ll success is voluntary. So is most failure. We lean toward the one we feel most permission for, regardless of what words we say or what others may think.

If there were actually one single unknown "secret" to explain why so many people fail to do or get what they want in life, it's this ignored ingredient I call *permission*. Not everyone has permission to succeed—not even believers.

Many silently affirm they are "born to lose," others that "nothing ever works out for me." Some get permission stolen from them (battered spouses, for instance, and families of alcoholics) by people who mistake themselves for God. Some act as if God made other people of better clay.

A handful are so dented by the doctrine of depravity, they see no hope of doing anything God-worthy while clothed in flesh, and sit like lepers outside the gate of life, scaring away others who might be willing to try to honor their Creator by using their gifts to seek success.

A few hesitate at the wrong moment in business. Others fear taking a chance or facing competition or the honest opinion of strangers. Their problem—and it is a common one—is not a question of preparation, belief, or faith, but simply of permission to succeed, free to be fully what God made them capable of being.

Lack of permission explains those people we see by the roadside of life, dressed for success, treasure map in hand, camped by the ditch—and going nowhere.

To them, it's a head-thumping revelation to learn that success eludes those who lack permission. They obeyed every "success rule" they could find, but no one ever told them about permission before. That's because nobody identified it before as a separate process. It's so obvious, it's invisible, though it's been in the Bible all this time, right before our eyes.

- Permission is a ritual or event that grants authority for a change in our behavior.
- Permission helps us believe we can achieve. It sets up our goalposts and fence posts, defining the boundaries within which we feel safe working.
- Permission falls somewhere on a line between hope and faith. It is the catalyst that turns hope into faith and unleashes faith's leverage power.

The Bible illustrates this by Christ's resurrection from the dead. His rising gave permission for His followers to believe, at last, what He so often promised: that He would rise—and that God could do the same for them. It took a miracle to make them believe. Finally, they understood that being born again meant being raised again too! The grave no longer was a one-way destination. This gave them permission for daring deeds, for their ultimate future, they saw now, was risk-free. To die was gain.[1] Why not dare great things for God? Why not make the most of their time on Earth? The world was never to be the same again, with people like these in it.

Before Jesus rose, the focus of life for the godly was downward, earthward, toward one's descendants and one's mortal grave, beyond which lay nothing, or nothing good. Personal survival after death was a blurry concept to the Jews of Jesus' time, who held differing opinions about it.

After Christ's resurrection, believers gained permission to look upward, heavenward, toward their personal resurrection to rule with Christ in heavenly places, and to their eternal life with a Father who loved them. Beyond the grave lay something better.

Resurrection meant the individual was important. The realization of this would change the world.

HISTORY'S TRUE WATERSHED

This shift in focus from the descendant to the ascendant changed civilization from that point on. The true dividing point of history is not the birth of Christ, as our calendars have it, but His resurrection. The promise of resurrection gave permission for new styles of behavior, for new patterns of living, for new hopes, new goals, new governments, and ultimately, new civilizations.

Until Christ rose nobody had permission for so audacious a faith as this: To believe ordinary people could actually depart the grave to live forever, or that the ultimate end of history would favor the good and the godly.

To us indeed Jesus gave permission to become the children of God. Children of privileged parents enjoy permission to expect more than others. God's children enjoy permission to expect and receive things like strength, guidance, wisdom, and protection. But we do not always use the powerful resources at our command. Like children who leave their jackets behind on cold days, we deny ourselves comfort and protection we have every right to claim.

Perhaps we lack permission to take God at His Word.

Stronger than outward faith, too often, is our latent belief that good things and happiness are "off limits" for us. We don't deserve them, we insist, and we continue to see ourselves the way God no longer does, as undeserving sinners. But we are His beloved children, once we've accepted His Son. God is not doing the forbidding here; we are, limiting our achievements by limiting our dreams. To some other person, inwardly authorized, the same blessings and benefits, self-forbidden to us, would pose no obstacle, becoming goals to power their success drive.

Permission is a basic human need. Without it we lack inner authority to act on what we believe to be true or hope is possible.

Few recognize this, however. If we saw people as automobiles, some could be seen fully fueled, engine tuned to peak performance, driver ready at the wheel, trunk loaded with dreams and aspirations—but parked in a garage, engine off, waiting for the garage door to open.

Waiting for what? A door to open! Permission!

They want a starter's pistol, some signal, sign, or go-ahead. They don't know what they wait for, only that they have no permission to leave the garage or take the high road to the success mapped out for them.

Without permission, our best talents cage us, our strengths bind us to the present, and we cannot escape to the future where our success lies. We stay locked behind self-closed doors, held back from the success God might enjoy helping us gain, by our fear and uncertainty. The person who seeks the blessing of God on a venture is asking for permission to succeed. That's a good start.

WHY THE WICKED PROSPER

The Permission Principle offers a hint why the wicked seem to prosper in their evildoing, a matter of frequent concern in the Bible. The ungodly live more dangerously than most of us, with less thought for the consequences of their actions. Being less inhibited, they require less permission before starting out on a course of action. It's one more restraint they do not have. They act before they think through.

Since lack of effort is a major reason people fail, a natural advantage befalls anyone who isn't slowed down by the need to call home for extra approval when an opportunity comes along. The wicked get while the getting is good. The godly may wait till the getting gets approved. They don't have to. Permission goes with the dream.

By sheer repetitive, brainless trying, the wicked—who need no permission, for they have little to hold them back—often succeed where good men don't. The lawless walk into opportunities created by those who left the door open when they went off to get a dose of permission and never came back. These good people would want permission to pick up diamonds unearthed in their own backyard.

BEYOND OBEDIENCE

Without permission, success is impossible, happiness unlikely. For if we venture to succeed without inward permission first, we often find ways to blamelessly bring our success crashing down around our ears. People who feel guilty about success have more success than they have permission for. Permission involves our inner authority to launch or continue actions that might result in success. (At some critical point, David and Jacob had permission; their opposites, Saul and Esau, did not.)

- Obedience applies to what we are told to do.
- Permission applies to what we want to do.

Some Christian believers get hung up on the obedience part and never get on to the permission part of God's plan for their lives, where success is found.

They live half-lives, looking for something further to obey, some final obscure commandment to fulfill, when all God hopes for by now is some voluntary good work from them after all their time in training.

Remember the parable in which the servant given money for safe-keeping fails to invest it?[2] While he was never told by his master to make the money reproduce itself, Jesus blamed the man for failing to invest the money WITHOUT BEING TOLD. Permission to use God's resources involves more than literal obedience, for the servant did (by burying it in a hole) keep the money safe, which was all he was instructed to do, and that was not good enough for Jesus.

While He expects our obedience in response to His love, He also expects us to make profitable use of our time on this earth, to be successful in some way, to the limit of our abilities—without being told. This success is not likely until we resolve our need for permission. Without permission, success is literally unthinkable.

POWER TOOLS

Lack of permission is a primary cause of "unexplainable" failure. We are as blind to permission as fish to water, as sinners to sin.

Some blame non-success on:

59

1) lack of enthusiasm, or
2) lack of clear goals, or
3) success being for "winners" only.

But more failures are caused by simple lack of permission—permission to succeed, to start up, or to persist in adversity—than by any other single thing. Without permission, progress grinds to a standstill.

When I started writing on the Permission Principle some years ago, being the first to do so, I had to define it in a few, simple words. This is what I said:

*Permission is a ritual
that grants authority for a change in behavior.*[3]

In an era that ritually denies the power of ritual, it is hard to make this point, but permission rituals underlie every human achievement since the evening our parents were thrown out the east gate of Eden and told to work for a living.

Our world runs on rituals of empowerment. The marriage ritual empowers us to expect reciprocal kindness from our mate and to produce children that everyone else recognizes as legally ours. If we enter government service we take ritual oaths to uphold the Constitution. When we don ritual uniforms as police or soldiers, we also clothe ourselves in permission to kill certain kinds of people without personal blame or punishment.

Important rituals are administered by those who represent systems of authority, such as clergy, magistrates, parents, and superiors. At times we administer them to each other, or to ourselves. It makes little difference the method, so long as we accept the new power that these permission-giving acts bring to our future.

When blind old Isaac bestowed his ritual birthright blessing on the wrong son, Jacob fled into exile to avoid his brother's rightful wrath but conducted himself henceforth like an elder son, favored of God and fathering all the tribes of Israel. He had permission.

After David's ritual anointing by Samuel, "Immediately the spirit of the LORD took control of David and was with him from that day on."[4] Taken into service as a part-time court musician, David soon was doing things a king should rightly do, which King Saul lacked the right spirit to undertake. Starting with his voluntary confrontation with Goliath, David acted ever the king, though it would be years before he became one in fact. He had permission.

Until the United Colonies rebelled against Mother England, most rituals—including clothing, wigs, and forms of address—enhanced class differences. This gave a few people permission to feel they were better than others and therefore in charge of all the money and power. The American Revolution overturned all this, which is one reason permission rituals remain thin in our society.

In a sense, the Declaration of Independence became one big permission-granting document, second only to the Bible in influence. While the American frontier was being settled, any homesteader could have quoted you Jefferson's phrase about "life, liberty, and the pursuit of happiness." It was part of every settler's kit of motivating ideas, which also included the family Bible.

It was the whole Bible, not just a few selected verses, that undergirded pioneers, to help them brave a hostile wilderness. Much of the Old Testament spoke to them directly, in terms of their immediate daily experience. They identified with all the texts that spoke of going to a far country to take possession of a promised land. They saw Native Americans as Amalekites and themselves as Israelites led by the hand of the Lord. In the Bible they found chapter, verse, and authority to "replenish and subdue the earth, and subdue it."[5]

In a word, the American pioneer had "permission" for his continent-conquering quest. He found it, he believed, in his Bible, God's Word, the handbook for strangers and pilgrims in a strange land.

Americans were not alone in this. The Protestant Dutch, who lost their New York settlements to the English, picked up their Bibles and settled the tip of Africa beyond the reach of British interests. While American pioneers wagon-trained westward, Dutch Boers carted themselves north from Capetown, both founding new nations in the process and finding permission for their actions in the same Scriptures.

PERMISSION BIASES THE FUTURE

Permission authorizes action to make our particular vision of the future the one others must live with, the one that history will record as fact. From a coldly secular point of view, the original inhabitants of North America and South Africa were swamped by settlers who believed they had permission to "subdue"[6] the earth. The tribes the settlers overran only believed in permission to cooperate with nature, or to placate her, not to challenge her. They lived as "children of nature" without thought of controlling the natural world (unless with magic) or wiping out the wilderness to build immense cities.

Permission is the difference between wishes and hopes that come to nothing and plans that succeed. We can't plan for what we can't conceive. We can't conceive what we have no permission to think about.

Our need for permission is rooted in fear of the unknown and in the way we are reared. From the moment of birth until we leave home for good, everything we do requires someone's permission. Is it any wonder we pass the portals of adulthood overly-aware of all we cannot do? It takes a long time to become truly grown up. A person of twenty-five has had eighteen years training as a controlled, permissionless child and only seven years practice being an adult. The sooner we get our permission in life, the sooner we can find our happiness and success, wherever it is.

Without permission's grant of authority to act, we stay stuck on "square one" of life, wherever we happened to land. We behave like those confused shoppers who step off a mall escalator and stop dead, staring about, undecided what to do next, until the moving staircase bumps a crowd into them.

Many people stay where they first land, fearful to move on without permission or instruction. One reason our East Coast is more crowded than the rest of the country is that so many who got off the boat simply did not travel very far.

OUR SOURCES OF PERMISSION

Conversion

In the Bible we find most of the permission-granting resources open to us today, including the most dramatic, spiritual conversion. Saint Paul turned his permission end-for-end in the three years following his dramatic conversion on the road to Damascus. Conversion came quickly; permission came slowly.

Prior to his encounter with Jesus, Saul of Tarsus was chief persecutor of the infant church. He rested that authority on documents from religious authorities in Jerusalem. They empowered him to bring Jewish Christians back in chains for trial. Later, he became chief propagator of the new faith, with the God-given authority of an apostle, one who has seen Christ and been sent out by Him to preach. Now Paul sought to release Jew and Gentile alike from the chains of sin and spoke of himself as the "prisoner of Christ" for their sake.[7]

Many churches point to a spate of similar life-inverting conversions in their history, exciting tales now enshrined in dull hagiographies (saint stories). Active congregations and evangelistic groups in our own time often know scores of such turnabout people in the flesh.

For some years I helped David Wilkerson, author of *The Cross and the Switchblade*, and his brother, Don, raise funds by mail for the original Teen Challenge ministry in Brooklyn. Every month I'd meet one or two new Christians of this 180-degree turnabout kind, won by street evangelism or neighborhood outreach programs. All had remarkable stories to tell of God's power in their lives.

Once drug addicts or alcoholics reduced to sleeping on rooftops and picking through garbage cans, they grew into radically changed, goal-directed people, redeemed, refurbished, and refocused by God. I have mental time-lapse pictures of some, seeing them grow, month by month, from cautious converts to committed Christians. Numbers went on to Bible school or other education, becoming pastors, teachers, and ministers, helping others trapped in their old lives without permission to escape.

Example

Part of the power of Teen Challenge and traditional rescue missions like Chicago's Pacific Garden Mission rests in the example of so many changed lives that come out of their work. Whatever doubters may say, all these people cannot be mistaken about what happened to them. In these hundreds of radically-shifted lives a Higher Power is clearly at work, and many others desperately crave the same experience for themselves.

Example gives people permission to change their lives. Sometimes it can give permission to end life as well. The example of the early Christian martyrs (martyr means "witness" in the sense of testimony)

65

has given permission for many since then to die, if necessary, for their faith.

As a footnote to the death of the first Christian martyr, the Bible mentions the role of St. Paul as a young man (Acts 7–8) in guarding the robes of those who stoned Stephen, a deacon of the Jerusalem church. Paul approved the killing, the Bible says. Stephen's example helped give Paul strength and permission to face his own martyrdom in Rome.

Example is one of the prime permission-givers to the young. What reader would be surprised to learn that my namesake uncle, Richard, was a writer too? Any model of family tradition, with father, uncle, sister, or aunt in a certain profession or business is enough to give a younger family member permission to follow a similar career.

Social problems result when this permission-model backfires, as it does when juveniles are jailed among older criminals. The example they receive from their jailhouse mentors, the record shows, gives too many permission for a life of crime.

Ceremony

Before written records, ceremonies were a standard way to imprint important events on the public memory so they would always be remembered. Wedding celebrations have always tended to a certain extravagance for this reason; everybody in the village remembers the day of the wedding and knows the two are married and the children theirs. Coronations and swearing-ins are rich with ritual and witnesses, so no one can question if they took place. Newborn princes are lifted ceremonially before the people to assure them the king has a successor.

Until our unceremonious age, authority, power, and permission were always communicated by ritual and ceremony. This tended to keep the authority base small and let those in control keep control. One could not do or attempt anything except with a writ of permission. Our American tendency to democratize privilege and everything else ruined that little game.

But rites still confer religious, social, and personal permission at important junctures of life. **Baptism** gives the Christian permission to enjoy the full life of the church and is a mark of a good conscience toward God.[8] **Communion** permits one to share inwardly in the life of Christ. **Ordination** confers permission to conduct the rites of one's faith and is a recognition of being set apart for God's service. **Funerals** originally were conducted to give the departing spirit permission to leave the premises for good, but now are recognized as part of the healing process for those left behind, as well as a "safe conduct" to the afterlife. **Weddings**, as we saw, confer mutual sexual permission.

Initiations permit new members to enter into all the benefits of a club or association. **Oaths of office** confer permission to pick up the symbols of a new duty and to wield the authority they confer. **Oaths in court** give permission to speak the truth of a matter to one's best ability. **Graduation ceremonies** give permission to leave an institution of learning honorably and confer symbols of achievement like degrees, which grant permission to employers to pay graduates a higher salary for special knowledge.

Signs

Permission for a specific course of action, in the Bible, is sometimes conferred or construed by "signs" from God. In the Old Testament these seem part of contract negotiations between God and the person involved, the sign being a confirmation of God's intention to that individual—and no one else.

We are nowhere given any list of signs that invariably mean God will do a certain, special thing when they appear. The Old Testament exception might be the rainbow as a sign of God's appeased wrath after Noah's Flood; next time the earth shall be purged by fire.[9] The New Testament exception, the "signs of the times" that will precede the return of Christ in judgment of the earth.

Gideon, fifth judge of Israel, sought a sign from God before consenting to lead the armies of his leaderless people against the Midianites. The specific sign Gideon bargained for had two parts. He put wool clippings on a flat threshing-ground and asked that dew make wet the wool and not the ground the first night. The second night he asked that the dew wet the ground and not the wool. This confirmed to him that God indeed wanted him to defeat the Midianites. Gideon obeyed and his people enjoyed forty years of peace.

Dreams and visions, again highly specific to the person and circumstance, appear frequently in the Bible, giving direction or permission for specific acts. Peter had a vision on the rooftop of Simon the tanner in Joppa which broke his resistance to preaching the gospel to non-Jews.[10] It gave him permission to associate openly with the ritually unclean Gentiles and open the gates of salvation to all.

Paul determined to take the gospel east into Asia—which would have made Western history and the world today much different from what it is—but received a signal to the contrary from God, to go to Europe.

> *That night Paul had a vision in which*
> *he saw a Macedonian standing and begging him,*
> *"Come over to Macedonia and help us!"*
> *As soon as Paul had this vision,*
> *we got ready to leave for Macedonia,*
> *because we decided that God had called us*
> *to preach the Good News to the people there.*
> Acts 16:9–10

By going to European Macedonia, as God directed, Paul evangelized the birthplace of the former Greek empire created by the son of King Philip of Macedon. The conquests of Alexander the Great reached from Macedonia, across Asia Minor all the way to India. Alexander's path was now a trade route linking these territories and on it Paul's gospel soon traveled eastward by caravan.

Westward went the same message with Paul to the capital of the

Roman Empire a few years later. Now he needed no sign to lead him, his presence in Rome being dictated by a legal matter.

Because Paul obeyed his heavenly vision, his personal sign from God, the course of history changed. He wanted to preach in Asia and head east. But being given permission to change his mind and shift his focus, he made the gospel to root itself deeply in both an eastward-facing and a westward-facing power center.

DRAWING STRAWS

Readers are sometimes puzzled to find references to "drawing lots" as a way of choosing between alternatives—getting permission to act—in biblical times. A trace of this tradition survives on our playing fields and in our courtrooms, where the toss of a coin may let chance break a tough fifty-fifty choice, by mutual agreement.

We are willing to accept that heartless Roman soldiers rolled dice for Jesus' seamless robe as He hung on the cross, for this fulfilled Old Testament prophecy. But it is troubling to think of the faithful apostles getting permission—God's approval—to cast lots to choose between two candidates to replace the fallen Judas Iscariot.[11]

To modern minds it does not seem that God should condone "spin the bottle" techniques to reveal His will to us. Were such the case, those seeking permission to start a new venture might do better with a dart board than an advisory board.

The culture of early times, however, made it easy to equate random chance with God's will. For could He not give the long straw or the short one to whomever He chose?

Maybe that's the answer we are stuck with. But it seems likelier what is described here in Acts was actually a vote. There were two candidates, Joseph called Barsabas and the man finally chosen, Matthias.

In their pre-selection prayer the Apostles said, "Lord, you know the thoughts of everyone, so show us which of these two you have chosen."[12] Their election was God's selection. Their collective mind would manifest in voting; the result was seen as God's choice. That's how it works in church council now. That's probably how it was then.

God expressed His intent through the minds and actions of His prayerful people, not by juggling the fall of the dice. Nothing has changed since then.

A PRAYER OF PERMISSION

The point for us is, we don't need to seek our "permission for success" in miraculous signs, visions, or dreams. We don't need them. Success is not a miracle. We can have permission for the asking. But we must have it.

If we cannot get outside authority to cut the restraining chain of permission for us, we can do it ourselves. Start by writing a prayer-memo like the one on the following page. Sign it, date it, and keep it with you to affirm, repeat, and remember in the days that follow. It can break the friction to get you going.

Lord, I thank You for Your love for me. I want
to serve You on Earth to my utmost,
without waiting for heaven
before I get started.

I believe that this strong desire
to make my days on Earth count
for more comes from You.

Help me to set and reach high goals,
measurable goals that will bless others
as well as me and my family.

I affirm, under You, my right, authority, and
permission as Your child to pursue to success
the godly goals You plant in me, that I might
use the fruits of success to bless Your people.

This could prove to be the second most important prayer of your life!

SUCCESS SUMMARY

✦ Permission authorizes new behavior, making success possible.
✦ Sometimes the wicked prosper because the good lack Permission to seize opportunity.
✦ Without Permission, success is literally unthinkable; we must have it.
✦ Permission is the first step to success. It goes beyond mere obedience.
✦ We can find our Permission to succeed by Conversion, Example, Ceremony, and even our own simple prayer of affirmation.

Permission goes with your mission in life. Don't delay starting your great venture, assuming some other person must approve it or you first. Scripture says God has plans for our prosperity (success) we know not of. With His plan comes His permission. Does anyone else's matter? Memorize Jeremiah 29:11.

Footnotes and Scripture references

[1] Philippians 1:21

[2] Matthew 25:14–30

[3] *Are You Positive*, 45

[4] 1 Samuel 16:13

[5] Genesis 1:28, KJV

[6] Genesis 1:28

[7] Ephesians 3:1

[8] 1 Peter 3:21

[9] Genesis 9:12–17

[10] Acts 10

[11] Acts 1:26

[12] Acts 1:24

SECRET
FIVE

$\mathcal{S}$uccess Comes After "Escape"

David ran away and escaped.
1 Samuel 19:10

$\mathcal{S}$uccess is not a ladder you climb to riches.

Success is a fire escape, a way out of a bad situation to something better.

Nor is success the start of winning; it is the end of losing.

English is not the best language to describe success. When an earlier book of mine was translated for distribution in Spain and Latin America, I learned something that has affected my work ever since. Their word for success is our word for fire escape—exit. (Spanish, success = *éxito*.) It's a helpful insight.

- Success is not the way UP, but the way OUT.
- Success is an escape, the exit from hard times.
- Success is getting out from under—NOT getting on top.

That success is an escaping of poverty and a way of leaving oppression behind is often overlooked. Without considering this aspect, some people reserve success for traditional "successful" role models (corporate executives, high-ranking officials, brilliant scientists, athletes, celebrities, and the like) to the exclusion of everyone else. Understanding success as one's way out of a disadvantaged past makes its circumstance-altering power available to more of us. Success—the escape of it—cures the past of wrongs.

Success is not given for us to dominate others, but to free ourselves from the domination and misused power of others, doing good things for ourselves and those important to us.

The Old Testament founding father Jacob was long and sorely misused by his father-in-law, Laban, who cheated him at every turn and changed his wages ten times.[1] Fed up, Jacob took his family, servants, and flocks one day and fled west. With Laban away on business, Jacob made his escape to the land of his fathers, where God gave him new prosperity.

Success, literally, can start with escape, breaking away from a past that holds us prisoner in some way. Often the prison is poverty. Not just money-poverty, but poverty of knowledge and of permission, as much as anything, imprisons us in the past to keep us from reaching our goals (which is all success means, after all).

SUCCESS WITHOUT LUCRE

Contrary to common lore, you do not have to worship mammon, the money-god, in order to succeed in life!

1) Success need not be linked to the Bible-banned love of filthy lucre.
2) Piety does not demand poverty to make God happy.
3) Money is not a requirement for every kind of success.

This is important to know, for this one false notion (that money equates with success) immobilizes much of God's investment in His people. He loads their genes with talents, gifts, and potential for God-honoring greatness, and many cower in a corner much of their lives, afraid to tap their talents for fear of success!

(Fear of failure, one could understand. But fear of success? Ask around if you don't think this concerns people. In my calling as a fund-raiser, I meet many sincerely religious people who shun achievement for fear it may turn them into Jekyll-Hyde money monsters. They are quick to tell you this; money scares them.)

This fear denies many who otherwise claim to trust God the full use of the potential He gave them for His glory and their good. Sideline sitters, they waste life's rich gifts in the strange belief that if they ever succeeded, they might not know how to handle the consequences and could lose favor with God.

They are willing to trust God to be poor, but not to trust God to be anything more.

To them, the Industrial Revolution never happened. Their attitude is to share poverty, not abundance. Abundance is a happy problem created by industrialization. They overlook two centuries of increasing abundance for ever-larger numbers of people since the mid-1700s—as if poverty were the highest good God expects anyone to attain. To them, anybody making money is tempting God to zap them down a notch or two. Success to them means only one thing—money. This is not the Bible's view.

Back when poverty was the universal reality and opportunity rare, Saint Paul wrote about the successful Christian life:

> *Make it your aim to live a quiet life,*
> *to mind your own business,*
> *and to earn your own living,*
> *just as we told you before.*
> *In this way you will win the respect*
> *of those who are not believers,*
> *and you will not have to depend*
> *on anyone for what you need.*
> 1 Thessalonians 4:11-12

Goals have not changed that much in 2,000 years. Whoever lives to Paul's standard today—minding your own business, earning your own living—attains as much success as most people could ever desire: self-sufficiency with God's blessing.

Success is something we each must define for ourselves. We each have different talents; we each find different success in developing them. There is no fixed outside standard for success. It is as individual as our God-given capacities.

Success, in part, is only another name for escape from bad things that keep us in bondage, things that bind us to painful pasts, things that keep us from blossoming and doing our best.

Money—always more money than we have at the moment—seems critical to success *only* because any lack of it limits our freedom to pursue new goals.

Money's critical absence keeps us imprisoned in the past. When we urgently need money, it is only for one of two reasons. Either we want to buy into a new future (investment) or buy ourselves out of past problems (pay off debt).

But money is not the only prison. For someone lacking education, the jail is ignorance. For those captive to the unjust power of a crippling person or circumstance, success can start only when they break the chains of guilt and escape. This may mean quitting a dead-end job or defying a dead-head boss, even starting your own business. Money may buy the hacksaw that gets you out, but it is not the measure of who you are.

Success is defined neither by the Fortune 500 nor the fortunate few. It is defined and agreed on between God and you. And it always starts with your escape from problems of the past.

DAVID'S ESCAPE TO SUCCESS

David, future king of united Israel, had many close calls escaping murder attempts by a mentally-ill King Saul, and finally fled over to the Philistine side and took refuge with the enemy, posing as a madman for self-protection. He escaped from Saul to save his life, but his running away also proved the turning point for his success in life. Shortly, he retreated to a cave outside a town called "Resting Place" (Adullah) and

When his brothers and the rest of the family
heard that he was there,
they joined him.
People who were oppressed or in debt
or dissatisfied went to him,
about four hundred men in all,
and he became their leader.
1 Samuel 22:1–2

Certain people burdened by their pasts escaped to join David, forming the core of an army that would one day acclaim him king. The escape to a cave did not mark the start of David's winning, but it did mark the end of his losing, for thereafter his cause grew ever stronger. He escaped his past and made his exit to the path of success.

(Note how closely success, as exit from a burdened past and escape to a new platform for achievement, reflects Bible teachings about forgiveness, God's way of helping His people escape the burden of sin to begin a new life.)

Great Biblical Escapes

The idea of escape figures so frequently in Scripture one could almost call the Bible the world's first "escape literature." One trait of these biblical escapes is that they always prove to benefit many others, as well as the escapee.

- Moses escaped to the desert after slaying an Egyptian, which lead to his encounter with God at the burning bush and return to Egypt to help his brethren escape their slavery.
- Jonah tried to escape from preaching doom in God's name by fleeing in a boat. He was swallowed by a sea creature, escaping death to preach God's message at Nineveh, where thousands repented, and their lives were saved.
- Noah escaped the Flood with his household and agricultural resources intact, to reestablish the human family on a cleansed earth.
- Joseph escaped death at the hand of his jealous brothers to live and rule in Egypt and to feed the Egyptian nation and his own family in a time of starvation.
- Another Joseph escaped to Egypt with Mary and Jesus to avoid Herod's decree of death for the infants of Judea.
- The Jewish captives in Babylon were told to "escape from Babylonia" and return to Jerusalem to build their temple and nation anew.[2]

- Early Christians, to escape rising persecution in Jerusalem, scattered as far as Cyprus, Syria, and North Africa, and new believers sprang up everywhere they went.

In the Bible, what starts out looking like running away—a personal escape from overwhelming problems—leads us to the other face of success, to new life, abundance, and prosperity. Success born of escape suggests we are sometimes better off not "standing our ground," but well served in leaving and finding ourselves new ground on which to stand and prosper.

WHY GOD ALLOWS SUCCESS

God has a reason for allowing, even encouraging, success. It is not so a few can lord it over the many, as some politicians tempt us to believe, hoping to make a legal grab at the successful's surplus to fund their power ploys.

The purpose of success is to help us escape hard times or to survive them.

Success generates rapid, lopsided abundance, a vital cushion against inevitable hard times. It gives us surplus to store. There is always a time coming when crops shall fail, markets collapse, wars break out, or plagues decimate the land. Mankind, except for God's mercy, is always dependent on what it put aside yesterday.

If God allowed no minority to strive for success, to make up for the fact that 95 percent of the population creates only 50 percent of the total possible wealth, there would be no "cushion" for anyone and no surplus to share.

Everyone would live in poverty, which is how the human race lived for most of history. All would be in danger of death from the next resource-stretching calamity. Success for the few is essential to the survival of all.

The business-successful are that vital minority—only five percent or so—creative in generating wealth in products, money, ideas, and services to the point that they outproduce everyone else nineteen- or twenty-to-one. They cause half of the wealth to come into existence. (And consistently pay roughly half of all income taxes.)

Without this super-productive minority, as the expired Soviet empire discovered, no nation can feed itself, much less aspire to world leadership. Society benefits from individual success that allows the few to feed the many, by providing jobs and building homes, cities, factories, and stores for all.

After his kingship began, David noted the improved economic condition of his people, the result of his personal success which began with the escape from Saul:

And so David realized
that the LORD had established him
as king of Israel

and was making his kingdom prosperous
for the sake of his people.
2 Samuel 5:12

By the successful actions of one person, a whole nation prospered. That's what success is all about and truly what it's for. Successful people make abundance possible for others.

ESCAPE GRANTS PERMISSION

In breaking the chains of a future-choking past, the "escape" aspect of success becomes a powerful stimulus to new achievement. Much of the success, energy, and off-the-scale achievement of America, compared to the rest of the world, can be explained by the stimulus of escape.

America was settled by escapees—people desperate to get out from under religious persecution in the Old World, potato famines in Ireland, anti-Semitism in Russia, poverty in the Orient, and militarism in Europe. Even if all our forebears ever did was escape to America, they became, by our definition, instant successes.

America, then, has a heritage of success. We were born to it. We understand it, tolerate it, and encourage it where other nations fear it. Our ancestors successfully escaped bad times and bad people, encouraging us later to become successful in every other way.

Back in David's time, once he escaped out of spear-reach of his quirky king, he could devote thought and planning to the survival of his nation, having no other responsibilities to burden him. He did not start out to fight Saul, but devoted his militia to driving out the Philistine marauders who made life dangerous for his people. Escape gave him time, resources, and permission to think and act like a proper king.

By dealing with the past—cancelling it if necessary by escape—the Bible's ideal of success frees us for the better future God is working through us. Without the past dragging, we are free to follow our vision of success and serve Him better. Success is our escape to something better, that which is best for us.

Success Summary

✦ Success is a better fire escape than a ladder to the top.
✦ The worship of money is not required for success.
✦ Success is something we must define for ourselves.
✦ The purpose of success is to provide for hard times.
✦ To escape the problems of the past is the beginning of success.

Standing pat and standing still can be wrongly read as standing firm or standing tall. The Bible does not advocate our standing on our past, but rather our escaping it—fleeing as much from our mistakes as from our sins. Israel did not find success as a nation until the Hebrew slaves escaped Egypt.

Scripture references
[1] Genesis 31:7
[2] Zechariah 2:6–7

SECRET
SIX

Success Builds on Vision and Goals

Where there is no vision, the people perish . . .
Proverbs 29:18, KJV

Success concerns itself with plotting an alternative reality, one more agreeable to our interests, to displace that which now exists. So, too, does much of our praying. We always pray for something better, not something worse.

The complaint is heard that "success promotes materialism." Upon reflection, it will be seen that sometimes it does, but only in the same sense that marriage promotes divorce and life is responsible for so much dying. Some "successful" people are materialistic, but that is neither the cause nor the necessary effect of their achievement. As we have seen, success is no miracle, but a phenomenon of the natural world that imitates the Creator's pattern of "disproportionate payoffs," a style that marks His handiwork wherever life is concerned.

Materialism has two meanings, and those disliking material rewards for the believer confuse themselves by linking the two. The primary meaning of materialism is that only two things—matter and motion—constitute the universe. Everything that is and that happens is due to the action of physical agencies only. This leaves no room for a God who intervenes in anything.

The secondary meaning runs on the human level, not the cosmic. Materialism here means the attitude of those who focus on material objects and material needs to the exclusion of spiritual values. They leave room for God, but an empty one. He is simply ignored.

The first says, "The physical is all there is." The second, "The physical is all I believe in."

Materialism is a normal road hazard on our pilgrim path, but not such a peril as to make all success-seeking a near-sin, as some do. It's something to be warned against, yes; something to pray about, of course. But no reason to pack up the picnic and go home hungry.

The fact is—and you can confirm this by skimming any "success book" you come across—most success writers explain themselves in spiritual terms, albeit sadly deficient ones if they are not Bible-believers. In this vein they attribute their personal success to a Higher Being, to spirit-guides, Universal Mind, "God as you understand Him," "your inner guide," or some-such, thanking a pale copy of the Bible's God for results they clearly cannot explain.

They never claim Newton's laws or Euclid's theorems or nuclear physics brought them success. Nothing so materialistic. If there are no atheists in foxholes, there are few in success books either. Far from being materialists, the successful generally assert that some invisible spirit-thing outside themselves is responsible for their super-productivity.

They lack enough Bible knowledge to know the right word for what's happened, but they rarely revert to materialistic explanations. They feel they've stumbled upon some law of life that gets results, and tend to mysticize it instead of rationalizing it.

Such writers are right to perceive success as spiritual law, not physical, but wrong to ascribe a miraculous aspect to it. Miracles require God's active intervention, an interruption or reversal of some natural process, but success does not require a divine thumb on the scale to make it work. Success is the positive side of the spiritual law: "As ye sow, so shall ye reap."

MATERIAL OBSESSION

Most arguments against success-as-a-hazard-to-your-soul are not seriously concerned with materialism in the primary, anti-God sense. It rarely happens. More common is obsession with material goods to the exclusion of a relationship with God, marked by a lukewarming of faith and backsliding from belief that God means what He says in the Bible.

On this subject a million sermons have been preached, so there is no need to preach another, only to draw a tighter conclusion: Don't avoid success for fear of wealth, but learn to use God's abundance properly. In other words, be a good steward.

Wherever the Bible rebukes the wealthy, read closely. Sometimes the complaint is *how* they got the wealth, sometimes it's *what they do* with it. Acquisition and use are the problems, not the wealth itself.

Money is power and, like all power, must be used wisely. Even the verse hurled at success-seekers more than any other—"Do not store up riches for yourselves here on earth"[1]—deals only with the selfish hoarding of resources. What is proscribed is not wealth itself, but selfish stockpiling of it.

"Instead, store up riches for yourselves in heaven" is how Jesus continued the thought, adding, "For your heart will always be where your riches are."

As an old country preacher is alleged to have said, "You can't take it with you, but you can send it on ahead." And that is the answer. The believer uses whatever resources fall under his temporary control to fulfill God's intent and meet peoples' needs.

Sometimes their need is for charity, but other times their needs are better met by good jobs, and it is up to the business-successful to invest riches to create them. This is better than charity because jobs help families to take care of themselves without reliance on others, the way Saint Paul said we should live if we possibly can.

Investing riches is not the same as storing them up.

Jesus was obviously talking against misers, not investors. Twice He spoke of moth and rust destroying riches and robbers breaking in to steal them. Clearly, this was idle money, selfishly locked away and kept from fruitful use by anyone.

Jesus did not fault the rich man who entrusted his wealth to his servants to invest while he was away. And the man punished the servant who was so dumb as to make the wealth useless by burying it out of money-fear, instead of investing it with benefit to both the owner and the user.[2]

This presents a fine example of the Bible's Disproportionate Reward Principle in how the returning master punished his "unprofitable" servant before throwing him out. He took back his two thousand uninvested coins and handed them to the more entrepreneurial servant who had turned his five thousand-coin stake into ten thousand, saying:

> *To every person who has something,*
> *even more will be given,*
> *and he will have more than enough;*
> *but the person who has nothing,*
> *even the little he has will be taken away from him.*
> Matthew 25:29

Here again is that recurring pattern of disproportioned rewards we keep seeing in our so-called Five Percent Rule. The erring servant offered back all that was entrusted to him, but could not placate the master, who expected the money to be earning in his absence, though he had not specifically said this to the servant.

Nor does God spell out all He expects from talents He entrusts to us. But it's obvious He expects gain. This brings us to the problem of success, also known as doing something useful with our lives. Success has two sides, public and private (or career success and family success). The truly successful succeed in both realms.

SERVING GOD IS NOT A GOAL

Many confuse their goals with their life-purpose, and this slows them down. They cannot be the same.

It is because we have purpose to our lives that we must establish goals. Strictly speaking, it may be a mistake to say our goal is to serve God, when we really mean this is our chosen purpose in life, our answer to His love. Serving God is a major life purpose, a purpose that remains unsatisfied if there are no objectives to fulfill it.

All true goals are characterized by being

1) measurable,
2) life-enhancing, and
3) very specific.

Serving God can never be measurable, for who can measure the worth of a human soul or the scope of God's wishes? And while God's service is life-enhancing, unless one is called upon to die for his faith, it is not very specific, because we have no way of reading God's mind in detail.

Upon our life's firm major purpose we erect the goals that make best use of our talents and opportunities in satisfying that purpose. Our Major Life Purpose is the ground zero of our success. The remaining steps are these:

1) Permission for success, the overlooked first step, over which so many stumble

2) Goal-Setting, in biblical terms, our "vision" of where we are headed with our life

3) Goal-Picturing or prayer in its capacity to change the future and help us see the new reality before it arrives

4) Goal-Striving (old-fashioned work), which leads us to the successful conclusion, that is, the

5) Goal-Achieving that motivated us all along.

The Climb to Success

"I win!"

God's Way
To Success

World's Way
To Success

	Work	5 Goal Reaching
	Prayer imaging	4 Goal-Striving
Vision of Future Desired		3 Goal-Picturing
Finding Authority for Success		2 Goal Setting
"Your Major Life Purpose"		1 Permission
		Firm Desire

SELF-FULFILLING PROPHETS

In one sense the successful are self-fulfilling prophets. They "see" a vision of a potential new future and by diligent work make it come to pass because they know it's up there ahead of them, waiting to be taken.

If anyone else bumped into the same opportunity, they might not recognize it in time to act, being unprepared for it by their lack of vision.

A goal is someplace you are going in your life by your own choice. It is where you desire to be or something you want to achieve. As such, it is like a beacon of light or a city set on a hill which cannot be hid. You lift your eyes to see it and instantly your daily choices are easier, for you can see your goal gleaming in the distance. Every decision becomes a step toward or away from your high goal. The right path is the one that reaches your objective.

Right goals simplify life. Others may plod aimlessly. You walk around them or past them, guided along your meaningful journey of achievement, led on by a vision of the future they cannot see unless you share it with them.

In the Bible, when servants of God like Daniel, Joseph, Paul, or Peter received a vision, it required interpretation before being acted on and always conveyed some special purpose God had in mind. In this way God's chosen servants got new goals to act on or special messages for others to act on. (The goals were originally God's, however, not theirs. They came with the job.)

Peter had a vision at the home of Simon the tanner, which symbolically said hereafter the gospel must be shared with non-Jews too, a new objective for the infant Church.[3] In a closely related incident the Roman commander Cornelius confronted a vision of a man in shining clothes before him, who said to send for Peter, who had for him a message from God. These visions led immediately to the first filling of Gentiles with the Holy Spirit. Only after all this took place did Peter fully understand his own vision.

Our visions are of a different sort than Peter's. Ours express personal hopes for the future in pictorial mental shorthand. They are no mystery, but born of our inmost desires, our intentions for the future.

By contrast, visions in the Bible are only for the purpose of revealing divine intentions to a particular person or group. While involving the same mental and spiritual mechanisms (if that is the word), these visions of the future have clearly different sources and purposes.

Seldom does a goal *kerplunk* itself into your life and say, "Take me, I'm yours." Usually we must sort through our dreams, experiences, and the models we see in life and in the Bible to extract goals that excite us most, then match them up to our "permission" file, which holds hints of what we feel allowed to try. Only then can we start to define our goals and let life move us on toward their achievement.

WHOSE JOB IS IT?

Some people try to skip this goal-choosing task, hoping to make God do it for them by insisting they simply want to "obey His will in all things." They figure if they let go of the steering wheel of their life—live dangerously devoid of all personal planning or goals to steer toward—surely God will make the choices for them and keep them safely on the road.

He may, but He's not obliged to.

"God's will" is not a catch-all phrase to glorify the living of an unplanned, unthinking life devoid of any goals of our own choosing. It means less than most people think. In the New Testament, God's will ("doing what God wants") has these restricted meanings:

1) For the unsaved person, what God wishes for them is to accept Christ as their personal Savior.[4]
2) For Christians, God wishes for them to live moral, clean, and dutiful lives.[5]
3) Elsewhere "God's will" is the phrase used to express hope for an uncertain outcome.[6]

Even if we assume God's will to mean simply obedience to His commands, success goes far beyond mere obedience, from conforming to transforming.

- Obedience is the *minimum* God expects from us.
- Success is the *maximum* God expects from us.

Why should God put us on earth to make choices (fundamentally, that's what we do here; think about it) and then make all the choices for us? Why not admit Creation was a mistake, cut out the middle man, and just do everything Himself? By the same logic a concert pianist must expect God to do his daily piano practice for him. Some things we just have to do for ourselves, and setting goals is one of them.

WILL YOU MISS GOD'S CALL?

Sometimes we get too pious for our own success—or good. Some see how God "calls" people to do special tasks for Him in the Bible and decide they must "wait upon the Lord" before making any serious choices in life, listening for a special message.

We're not talking about sensible praying for God's blessing and direction. We're dealing with major inactivity here, pulling the caravan to the side of the road and setting up camp permanently in the ditch unless God sends a satisfactorily spine-tingling message to gird up their loins and get going. They "read themselves" into the Bible as characters in it, instead of reading examples out of it.

What is overlooked is the truth that God never "calls" idle people to help Him. He always interrupts busy people at their work. He just plain butts in on them. He persists and won't let them go until they agree to do what He says. (If any said no, they never made it into the biblical record.)

The chart on page 103 pretty well shows the Bible pattern.

102

God Never Calls an Idle Person

Person called	When called was busy
Moses	Herding sheep
Gideon	Threshing wheat
Samuel	Guarding ark as he slept
David	Tending sheep
Elisha	Plowing with oxen
Nehemiah	Serving the king
Simon & Andrew	Fishing in lake
James & John	Readying nets
Matthew	Collecting taxes

God can redirect you if you are in motion

Here's the point: If God wants to tap us for special service, He is more likely to call on us if we're busy at our daily task than if we're waiting for an angel to ring the doorbell.

We won't miss out on God's call in our lives just because we decide to work toward our goals. It keeps us busy for a good purpose. God can interrupt any time He needs us. He is not bashful. The added blessing is that in responding to some need He presents to us, we often move closer to reaching our own goals. If our Major Life Purpose is to serve God's purposes, no matter what happens we can't lose.

ALTERNATIVE REALITIES

In the Bible, God usually selects an "alternative reality"—the fork in the future He prefers that history take—by choosing one person whose grafted goal it becomes to make the future turn out God's way. He never starts with an army or with a crowd, only with one solitary individual whose sole advantage is that God gave him a goal.

Only rarely does God directly intervene and alter history Himself, without the hand of man. When He does, it is recognized as an act of divine judgment, as was Noah's flood, the confusion at Babel, and the destruction of Sodom and Gomorrah.

The prophet, king, or spiritual leader God chooses to rewrite history before it happens always retains his or her own will but has personal goals replaced, by consent, with those assigned by God. Since God cannot fairly force our wills without making us into puppets, we see contradictory behavior in the lives of many biblical characters when their personal will and God's superimposed goals do not stay merged.

- Despite all the good David did for God's people, he arranged for the death in battle of one of his faithful followers so he could enjoy the man's wife.[7]

- Likewise, after Gideon's small band soundly defeated the enemy army in Jehovah's name, he took forty pounds of captured gold jewelry, melted it into the shape of an idol, and set it up in his hometown to be worshiped by God's people.[8]

This tension between will and goals affects every success-seeker, which is why we should match the push of our will and the pull of our goal as closely as possible. In biblical times, unlike the present, God always imposed a specific goal upon each person He called to serve Him.

- Noah's assigned goal was to "replenish and subdue the earth"
- Abraham's, to father multitudes as the family of God
- Moses', to lead God's people to the Land He promised
- Joshua's, to take them into the Land
- David's, to create and lead a strong and united kingdom
- Solomon's, to build the Temple of God

Even Jesus, fully human and fully God, with the goal of salvation for mankind, had to converge and merge His own will with the Father's as he prayed before His crucifixion.

Three times He prayed at Gethsemane:

My Father, if it is possible,
take this cup of suffering from me!
Yet not what I want, but what you want.
Matthew 26:39

As God's Son He knew the goal and had agreed with it from the foundation of the world. Still, at His darkest hour, He had to work at bringing His own will on Earth into line with the heavenly purpose.

What does all this mean for the rest of us?

It means that while God may imbue us with a Major Life Purpose, He leaves to us the discovery of specific goals that will accomplish this. It's called free will.

Only to a few special people at special biblical times did God command a specific goal be reached. And always with that goal He supplied miracles and whatever else they needed to reach it.

Not so with us. We set our own goals; we make our own way, with God's help, but with no assurance of miracles to ease our way. Instead of guaranteed miracles, we get something almost as good—spiritual laws that work the way physical laws do, at all times and all places, for all persons. The spiritual laws of success, as we saw, start with the equation that we reap what we sow.

THE BIBLE IS NOT ABOUT US

Times of imposed goals and assured miracles (divine intervention)

106

are so rare as to be written up in the Bible for their teaching value. Today, outside Scripture, we need to go slowly around people who insist God gave them a specific goal to accomplish, for by rights, miracles should come packed in the same box with any God-given goal and not require help from the rest of us.

God is not the author of confusion. Anybody who is not written up in the Bible must identify and work out his own life-goals, not expect God to impose His.

The Bible is FOR us, not ABOUT us. To argue that we must do something (e.g., expect God to assign our goals) "because it's in the Bible," is not valid. Even persons known for their faith and devotion to the Bible avoid patterns for which there are ample examples in the Scriptures—concubinage for instance.

Dream interpretation figures widely in the Old Testament as a way of discerning the mind of God. Yet what church today offers Wednesday Night Dream Interpretation Meetings? We have the mind of God already, more than we can handle in a lifetime, in the Bible. They did not.

Since the Bible offers a revealed religion, not a man-made one, of course God found it necessary to impose special goals on those He chose to help Him! Their own would not have led them to the truth in a thousand years! Because He had to impose goals on Peter, Paul, and Moses does not mean He must impose them on us.

THE LIMITS OF GOALS

In setting the goals that define "alternative reality" (the future according to our hopes), we literally set outer boundaries on our intended success—even on our life itself. Each goal we choose is a fence post on the border of our being. Unless success or disaster—or a personal decision—forces a breakthrough that brings new objectives into our lives, we will never move beyond these goals.

The word *goal* is rooted in the Anglo-Saxon term for boundaries, like the bounds of one's village. Most people live within a self-erected fence of limited goals all their lives. God didn't say they had to do it. They chose it. But as we are discovering, the Bible says it is really okay to have success goals if you can do it in a Christ-honoring way.

Most of us need to move our fence line, our goals, further out to the horizon, where they can touch heaven.

Most chokes on achievement come from inside, not outside. If we fail to set worthy goals, we cannot blame our parents, our spouses, our siblings, our environment, or anyone for any lack of success. And we can't excuse ourselves or blame God by saying He chose not to do miracles for us.

Success does not require miracles. It works by spiritual laws that demand goals first.

Our success—the alternative reality we choose—is built upon goals we ourselves select and then envision in strong detail, as the next chapter explains.

SUCCESS SUMMARY

+ Success concerns alternative reality, the version of the future we most desire.
+ Success requires us to be good stewards.
+ Success is built on our Major Life Purpose, led by goals.
+ The successful are "self-fulfilling prophets" who see goals clearly.
+ Obedience is our minimum, success our maximum service to God.
+ Goals mark boundaries of ambition and achievement.

> *The world laughs at "dreamers" like Joseph. But he became the most powerful citizen in Egypt because **his dreams had numbers on them**— seven fat years, seven lean years. Any vision of the future lacking numbers is a taunting dream, not a measurable goal.*
>
> *What was the first thing Moses did after coming off Mount Sinai? He took a census—he numbered God's people!—before they went off to seek success in the Promised Land. See Numbers 1:2.*

Scripture references
[1] Matthew 6:19–21
[2] Matthew 25:25–27
[3] Acts 11:16–18
[4] Matthew 7:21–23
[5] Ephesians 6:6; 1 Thessalonians 4:3
[6] Acts 21:14; Romans 1:10
[7] 2 Samuel 11:1–17
[8] Judges 8:26–27

*G*oal-led faith
will find
windows
where
blind faith
feels for walls.

SECRET SEVEN

Success Follows Faith and Faithfulness

To have faith is to be sure of the things
we hope for . . .
Hebrews 11:1

If, then, you have not been faithful
in handling worldly wealth,
how can you be trusted with true wealth?
Luke 16:11

$\mathcal{B}$ible readers have created more wealth than any other people on earth. At the same time, they have generated more happiness and hope than any in history.

Despite the problems of our planet, its overplus of population and large pockets of poverty, the fact remains that today more people are alive, well-fed, adequately housed, and educated than ever in human history. Lay this at the door of the people of the Book who found in the Bible a simple life-organizing idea that led them to new abundance while all their neighbors were going in circles.

In presenting a God who writes contracts with His people, the Bible concerns itself with beginnings and endings, which all contracts require to frame the times the parties are to be bound. This reveals something to us about the nature of time as God created it, something important to all success and happiness.

The Bible shows us a God who created *time* as linear, not curved, a straight line and not a circle. You may think this only common sense, but not many cultures see time the way we do, as a consumable, unrecyclable commodity. They see time as a wheel to which suffering mankind is shackled for endless cycles of repeated—and therefore meaningless—events. If history thus has no meaning, neither then does life in general nor ours in particular. Any idea we have of trying to make life better is a waste of time. The sooner life is over the better, according to them.

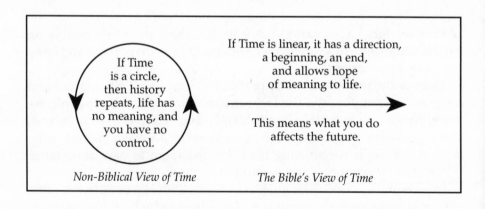

If Time is a circle, then history repeats, life has no meaning, and you have no control.

Non-Biblical View of Time

If Time is linear, it has a direction, a beginning, an end, and allows hope of meaning to life.

This means what you do affects the future.

The Bible's View of Time

But from its opening phrase in Genesis 1:1, which marks the official start of time on earth, to its last joyful prayer of blessing in Revelation 22:20–21, waiting for Jesus and the end of time, the Bible shows time running in a straight line with its length known only to God.

Therefore the past is not to be revisited but requited. We are each held responsible for what we do, since judgment is coming on the last day of time. History does not rotate on a wheel of karma or helpless destiny. It is headed somewhere. And one day time shall end, when God says so.

This simple idea—that time runs in a straight line headed in a meaningful direction—yanked pessimism out of the human future and made all progress possible. We did not stay trapped in caves and tents. We each got some control over what we achieve here on earth. Our rewards and punishments are those we earn.

This means you and I personally need not repeat the problems and failures of our parents. (Though many, lacking other permission, do so.) If Uncle Willie was a drunk or Grandfather was a horse thief, that does not mean we have to be like them.

What the Bible did to free the ancient world, it does for you and me today, offering us alternative futures, focused on goals, instead of a bleak, recycled past. As we shall see, the concept of a flexible future, one that can be made different by what we think and do today, is vital to the idea of success.

A determined pessimist can still make a case for the devil by running a straight line from the past into the future, as the next diagram shows.

This flat track is for people without personal goals or plans, without hope, but mostly just without permission. They must take what comes. If life were tennis they would never get to serve.

Others, using their permission to choose, know the future can be bent any way they want, simply by establishing a new "attraction point" in the future—a specific, measurable, life-enhancing GOAL.

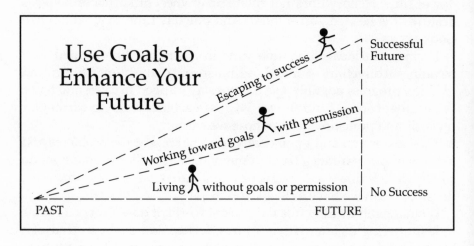

With a powerful new goal as attractor (*Goal B or C*), *our future is tugged upward along a hopeful new path, away from the fatalism of those without permission to have a say in their own lives.*

THE FORGOTTEN FACE OF FAITH

The reason for looking at the nature of *time* is that *faith* is a function of time and not of eternity. *Time delivers what faith foresees.* Faith runs along the corridor of time and concerns itself with seeing now—and relying on today—the fulfillment of events yet in the future. When time is no more, faith will no more be needed. Everything promised will have been delivered.

Heaven is for those who have been faithful. Success is for those who have faithfully pursued their goals. Their faith sees across time's gap of tomorrows to the goals that beckon them onward. Faith, like happiness, becomes a continuing attitude of joyful anticipation, whether of goals achieved or Heaven reached.

The Bible perfumes its idea of faith strongly with a scent of sweat. Faith in the Bible is work, not stress-free daydreaming. It was no easy faith that led Job, in his physical and emotional agony, to say, "Though He slay me, yet will I trust in Him."[1]

Faith works hard, for it must see through, beyond, and around the tangible obstacles and problems that are the only things outsiders see when they look at us. Others see the work and not the reward. Until we reach our goals, few of them understand who we really are, or what our faith has made us become.

The wonderful secret about our problems, by the way, is this: Unlike a question, which has but one answer, problems have many answers. Goal-led faith will find windows where others find walls. The Bible

119

may give us but one way to Heaven, but grants us many paths to success.

Like infrared goggles that let us see—after a fashion—in the dark, faith lets us see in rough outline the future, at least the parts of it in the vicinity of our goals. Just as memories give us "feedback from the past," so goals (through the faith that planted them there) give us "feedback from the future." Feedback, as error-correcting input, gives current information about events to help us keep moving accurately toward a goal.

WHAT FAITH MEANS

A word used a great deal sometimes builds up a meaning that is not quite what the original users had in mind. Faith is such a word. In religious contexts today, faith has shaded itself to have a dominant meaning, which is not the primary meaning of the word in the Bible.

Modern speakers talk of faith as if it meant primarily "intensity of belief" (as in, "She's a person of great faith"). Bible readers may give more weight to what is being believed and emphasize the ideas of hope and trust (as in "Have faith in Christ"). These are proper meanings, but there is another aspect to consider.

When we use the word *faith*—especially in the area of goal-setting—we need to remember that in the Old Testament *faith* and *faithfulness* appear most often in the sense of being steady, stable, and steadfast.

The person deemed faithful was extolled for consistent, persistent, and invariably praiseworthy behavior in regard to something good. This is identical to faith as we display it in pursuit of our goals.

While trace elements of truth and hope are alloyed in our faith, it is the iron in our souls—our steadfastness and stability of behavior—that comprises the real meaning of faith for our purposes.

We should have faith in our goals, or why else would we have chosen them? This is faith in its sense of belief, hope, and trust. Success is as much concerned, however, with faithfulness in its sense of endurance, which is what it takes to see us along our journey to success.

PRE-VISION AND PROVISION

Jesus said those who act upon their firm belief in getting what they pray for will get it.[2] It is in the act of showing ourselves prepared for the goals we pray for and work for that we start to receive them. Like the birth of a new baby, our successes should not be a surprise when they finally arrive. Success must be believed in to the point that we prepare for it, even when the outward evidence does not suggest it to be plausible.

The book of 2 Kings offers a powerful example of preparation for a solution that seems implausible. The people's anticipation of the good to come by preparing for it is an act of practical prayer, calling for a stronger faith than mere word-prayers.

The story is this. A Jewish king and two of his allies joined in war to punish the king of Moab, whose kingdom lay off the southeast quadrant of the Dead Sea. They elected to attack from the south, along the Great Rift Valley that cradles the saltiest lake in the world, and in doing so marched through hot, stony, waterless desert. After marching seven days they ran out of water and had none left for themselves or their pack animals.

One of the kings asked if there wasn't a prophet around who might tell them what God intended to do (a little late to ask, one thinks), for otherwise they were helpless if the king of Moab should attack. They went to see Elisha and he told them,

This is what the Lord says:
"Dig ditches all over this dry streambed.
Even though you will not see any rain or wind,
this stream bed shall be filled with water,
and you, your livestock, and your pack animals
will have plenty to drink."
2 Kings 3:16–17

The next morning, "water came flowing from the direction of Edom and covered the ground."[3] They were saved. And because they prepared by digging ditches, the fast-moving floodwaters were trapped long enough to supply the army for its campaign. In fact, had the flood not been expected, the three kings and their army could well have drowned.

(In the same region today, tour buses sometimes get swept away when flash floodwaters cross low spots in the highway. They wash down from cloudbursts over distant parts of the Great Rift Valley badlands.)

Now at this point the story gets even more interesting. The kings sought God's mind because their lack of water made them vulnerable to military attack. "The LORD has put the three of us at the mercy of the king of Moab!" is how verse 10 puts their panic. They hadn't asked for help in beating the Moabites, but they got it.

As the soldiers went about digging holes in dry dirt, Elisha said

But this is an easy thing for the Lord to do;
he will also give you victory over the Moabites.
2 Kings 3:18

Sunrise found the Moabites alert on the frontier, waiting for the three kings to advance against them. Then they fell victim to optical illusion and self-delusion. Red sunlight reflecting off pools of receding floodwater convinced the Moabites they were seeing the spilt blood of the three armies, which must have quarreled in the night.

The Moabites broke ranks, lost discipline, and rushed down to loot the supposedly defenseless invaders' camp. When they reached it they were attacked and driven back. The invaders then pursued them and ravaged the land.

The original goal of the kings had been to punish Moab. Their human need dictated a second goal—getting water first. Told by God's man that water was coming and they must prepare for it by digging holding ponds in the dry washes, they believed and obeyed him. They expressed their faith with two hands and the humble digging stick every soldier carried for personal latrine duty.[4] This work proved a most effective prayer, for not only did the water come to them, so did the enemy, in disarray, defeated in advance.

Believing in our goals to the point of acting upon them as though they are real already is the ultimate test of our faith and our faithfulness. And the ultimate trigger for their realization when the time is right.

THE SPILLOVER FROM BELIEF

Sometimes when we act in faith upon a sincere belief, be it a belief in our someday success or the certainty a Bible promise shall be fulfilled in a way that affects us, amazing things happen.

Perhaps none more amazing than the fact that our entire mechanical culture, from spacecraft to sewing machine, satellite television to lawn mower, can be traced to one sincere belief of the early church—that Jesus would return soon.

If you trace backward through the files of the United States Patent Office to its beginnings, then read the early scientific journals published by learned societies in England, then scan the libraries of the great universities of Europe founded in the Middle Ages, then do some industrial archaeology back into late Roman times, you find the heritage of the modern machine age. The father of it all—or should we more aptly say the grandfather—was the mechanical clock.

Clocks became the first powered mechanisms not run on the energy of animals, water, or wind. From clock-making came the skills and ideas which led by one path and another to our modern technology.

Yet it was the religious motivation of the early church, and monks subsequently, that created a market demand for clocks, a technology that could tell time. (That is, count time the way bank tellers count money.)

Why were these early Christians the first people in history to care exactly what the hour was? Empires had flourished and faded for millennia up to this point, with nothing more accurate to tell their time than a sundial or primitive water clock. The monks craved better timepieces because of some words by Jesus recorded in Matthew:

> *. . . You must always be ready,*
> *because the Son of Man will come*
> *at an hour*
> *when you are not expecting him.*
> Matthew 24:50

They believed Jesus was coming back, as promised in the Bible, at an unknown day and hour. As good servants, they wanted to be awake, ready to serve Him, whatever time of day or night He came.

Someone was always fully dressed and on duty in the chapel all night, ready to greet the Bridegroom should He appear. (Fear was an added inspiration. They remembered too the parable of the unprepared persons who got locked out when the Bridegroom returned unexpectedly.)[5]

To keep track of each hour and rotate each man's turn of watchful waiting by the altar, they started looking for means to measure time accurately. Though it took centuries, this need led to the invention of striking clocks that announced the hour.

Christendom's early swing into mechanical technology reveals itself even today. If you spend the night in an East Jerusalem hotel, you are awakened pre-dawn by two sounds—a voice and a bell.

The voice belongs to a Muslim muezzin at a hillside mosque calling Allah's faithful to prayer. The bell peals forth from a church on the nearby Mount of Olives, a relic of the long tradition of marking the hours so one could be ready for Christ's return.

To follow the sequence one step further, the metallurgy which grew up to make church bells turned out to be the same as that needed to cast cannons. So when gunpowder came to the West from China, where it was used mostly for firecrackers and skyrockets, the means lay at hand to develop artillery. Cannons soon made castle walls and moats obsolete and this led to the end of the feudal system. And so on.

This lengthy excursion outside the Bible to make our point is justified for one reason. It shows the amazing way one small group's continuing faith and faithfulness about the Bible changed the world for everyone forever.

It is still that way. We may never know the final effect of our efforts—on ourselves or the rest of history—as we set out to achieve our goals. But it is clear that our faith and faithfulness will take us beyond mere success.

SUCCESS SUMMARY

+ The future is flexible, waiting for us to shape it.
+ Faith both sees and relies today on the fulfillment of events in the future.
+ Faith finds windows where others find walls.
+ Faith is as much concerned with steadfastness as with hope.
+ Effective faith spills over and blesses others as well.
+ Practical prayer—acting in faith upon belief—is stronger than word-prayer.

> *The future is not inevitable. It can be changed—either by us or someone else. The successful are those whose alternative version of the future comes to pass. Success and prayers alike are both concerned with making the future agree with our desires.*

Scripture References
[1] Job 13:15, KJV
[2] Mark 11:24
[3] 2 Kings 3:20
[4] Deuteronomy 23:13
[5] Matthew 25:1–13

APPLYING THESE SECRETS IN THE REAL WORLD

Success Model—The Exodus from Egypt

Then the LORD said to Moses,
"Go to the king and tell him that the LORD says,
'Let my people go . . .'"
Exodus 8:1

A biblical model of our success is the Exodus.

The collective escape of the Hebrews out of Egyptian slavery and their settlement as a free people after crossing the Jordan many years and adventures later can be read as a metaphor of our personal struggles for success.

Admittedly, this modern concept was never in the mind of the inspired writers, but the success allegory is easily seen. As we say, each generation finds new treasures in the Bible. This is one of its truths emphasized in our time.

Seen this way, the Exodus tells this tale:

- A people meant for greater things fell into economic bondage.
- The harder they worked, the less they got to show for it.
- Hard work was not the way out of their slavery.
- God gave them new hope of success—*i.e.*, goals of personal

achievement and rewards (the very opposite of slavery)—to be earned in freedom under Him.

- God sent a person of vision to lead them to a place where inspired belief was rewarded and success was possible.
- They escaped their burdened past in seemingly miraculous ways.
- In a time of inspiration, they acquired new standards for living.
- In a time of testing, the doubting and the fearful fell by the wayside.
- Those who persisted reached their goals and were blessed by God.
- Even those who did not reach their ultimate goal, like Moses, who died before crossing the River Jordan, had at least lived on life's highest plane and prepared the way for their successors' success.

Traces of the Exodus experience linger in our language, frozen in phrases and hymns that dwell on "crossing over Jordan"—our metaphor for dying.

The image of the Exodus as an allegory of life's struggles with justice and rewards postponed beyond the river of death spread in the spirituals sung by black Americans in slave times. Their imagery reflected hope for a better life beyond the grave, if nowhere else.

BREAKING AWAY TO THE FUTURE

As the American Revolution is the defining experience of our nation, so the Exodus defined the "peoplehood" of the Jews forever. They had entered the lush lowlands of Egypt as economic refugees 430 years earlier, Jacob and his band of seventy. Twenty generations later, they departed, a nation six hundred thousand men strong, plus women and children, a population larger than inhabits any of a half-dozen of our smaller states today.

Their sheer fecundity shows they prospered. Prosperity, as we know, is the Bible word for success. As often happens, success makes others jealous. The new king hoped to divert to his own uses the energy that made the Jews prosper amidst the envious Egyptians. Today a wicked political force might use taxation to this end, to oppress a minority. Pharaoh chose to use forced Jewish labor, as Hitler was later to do, hoping to work the people he hated to poverty and extinction. Both had similar personal motives—neither would tolerate another's success if it meant freedom from their selfish control.

OTHER LESSONS FROM THE EXODUS

Think about that sometime, when you find strong opposition to your going off and achieving something on your own. Ask yourself why some person is upset at the prospect of your success. Usually it's a matter of control.

Lesson One from the Exodus is that your success may not endear you to others. Be prepared for this—and be prepared to move on to find greater success, elsewhere, leaving them behind.

The march to Canaan took forty years, during which the tribes were tested and found wanting. It was good they already had a contract with God or He might have given up on them because they were so rebellious and unbelieving.

Their migration ended effectively in two years, but the people balked on the border of Canaan, afraid to exercise enough faith to cross over, so God put them in a holding pattern of wanderings for thirty-eight years, while the balkers died.

Only Moses believed the optimistic minority report of the spies Joshua and Caleb, two of a dozen sent to spy out the land for invasion. The two insisted military victory was possible. The negative ten-man majority report, misleading and scary, fit the fears of the crowd. Theirs was like some news media reporting in our time which deals in fears and half-truths to build attentive audiences they can sell to advertisers.

Faith-suppressing fear is not without cost. God's chosen people, choosing to hold onto their fears rather than practicing trust in His promises, needlessly denied themselves the blessings of a homeland for thirty-eight years. This evildoing was not the work of some enemy. It was self-inflicted by their doubts.

Nothing made their homelessness inevitable other than failure to entertain any self-image of themselves succeeding in the land—even aided by God's promised presence and blessing. Like many today, they felt God might be trusted to help them in poverty, but never in times of plenty. So they deflated high expectations from life, foreseeing disaster as the price one pays for trusting God for more than the barest necessities. They lived with little, to avoid trusting God for more.

What we think about ourselves is important. We are not to despise God's creation—ourselves. If we are not to think too highly of ourselves, neither are we to think too little. Moses' generation chose to wallow in poverty-assuring mental self-imagery—describing themselves as "grasshoppers" as compared to giants rumored to be found across the river in Canaan.[1]

Even an oversized grape cluster—so large Joshua and Caleb carried it back on a stave between them—was read as a bad omen. The two spies took it to demonstrate the fertility of Canaan's soil and to show that the Canaanites could not protect their own property. But to the fearful, oversized grapes meant one thing—giants must have planted them! God's abundance was fear-read as proof of giants in the land.

Bad self-imagery breeds bad consequences. *Lesson Two:* We tend to become what we see ourselves being. We are either grasshoppers or giant killers. And we choose which.

God did not argue with the people. He let Joshua and Caleb do that. They did their best to halt a full-scale rebellion in which the people threatened to kill Moses. Over what? Over their insistence that God could not be trusted. He had brought them all that way just to kill them!

It is one thing to move forward into empty desert or to follow the person ahead of you across dry sea floor, with the war chariots of Pharaoh at your heels. Whether it's fear or faith at work is hard to say when safety lies ahead and danger behind.

It is quite another thing to move forward across an enemy border with only God's promise of success urging you on. Positive faith is called for. The only faith the rebels displayed was negative. They believed the opposite of what God said.

Once again we see people choosing to be poor—and working hard to keep themselves that way—by doing everything they can to avoid trusting God for something better! They had a valid contract for possession of the land, yet refused to move in.

BURYING FEARS THE HARD WAY

In the end, Joshua and Caleb were the sole remnant of that unbelieving generation to enter the land "flowing with milk and honey." The soft Egyptian-born cohort died flexing the biceps of its well-exercised fears. Forced by lack of self-belief to dwell outside the place where God promised them success, they lived out their shortened days in wild places, their feet sore from tramping useless circles in the sand.

After their rebellion against Moses, God spun them 180 degrees away, far from the green banks of the fresh-water Jordan, to the salty Gulf of Aqaba, one of the more lunar-looking places on earth. At least there were no reported giants in that vicinity.

This fear of tall enemies haunted them for hundreds of years. How often we do the same thing ourselves, halting at the brink of success, fearing others we know of only by report, who are supposed to be taller, better, more talented, or more deserving than we. *Lesson Three:* It is not reality that stops our success so much as our giant fears. *The fearful quit because of something small inside, not something big outside.*

Though a new generation crossed the River Jordan, it would be centuries more before God's people came into effective possession of the land that was theirs already by contract. Centuries later, once David slew Goliath—the most famous of all Canaanite giants—the people found no problem killing off any other giants that lurked in the land. The example of the first successful person is always quickly acted on by others who hesitated till then. Success breeds success.

But in their days of wandering the mere report of giants was enough to scare a people away from success the rest of their lives. Yea, better to endure familiar privation as homeless persons without regular employment, struggling to raise kids in a poor environment and with no inheritance to give them, than to take any chance of your fully-weaponed army encountering some solitary stringbean genetic fluke in a bronze suit across the border. Yea, verily.

Lesson Four: Despite miracles, the Israelites did not "see" themselves successful, so they never were.

What they felt inside overrode what they saw God doing outside.

It mattered not that they were the generation who witnessed the greatest miracles of any in the Bible. They had survived the dread night of Passover when the angel of death took the firstborn male in every family not protected by a blood-marked doorpost. They had seen the mighty plagues of locusts, frogs, gnats, flies, and polluted water God had sent upon the Egyptians. They were there when the Red Sea walled itself into a dry walkway for their orderly retreat before the king of Egypt and his chariots, upon whom the waters fell in.

They had been there, had seen it all. None of this was secondhand knowledge or a passed-on tale. For years they were led daily by the Shekinah, the visible Presence of God with Us, and fed each morning by manna they had only to pick off the ground. If living surrounded by—and benefitting from—spectacular miracles could make a people do the right thing, this surely was the generation to whom it should happen.

But it did not.

Perhaps it was the slave experience, but something dented their spirits, denying them permission to succeed as conquerors of Canaan, even with the Lord Our Banner to lead them. They lacked the forward vision of the success-minded, having an overdeveloped rearward vision—glamorized memories of the "good old days" in Egypt, where there were leeks and onions and garlic to eat—forgetting they were enjoyed in chains.[2] A taste for the past killed their foretaste of a better future.

SUCCESS LIES NOT IN THE PAST

The successful are always people of the future. The original Israelites were not that, though their field-hardened children were. The young's vision of a future of their own making, blessed of God, was not spoiled by competing memories of the past or distracting visions of failure. As we saw in the chapter on success as escape from failure, problem-filled pasts are baggage to be left behind if we are to achieve new dreams and goals.

The generation enjoying the most direct contact with God had the least belief in His promises. They survived, but did not find success. It would remain for descendants with no guiding pillar of cloud by day and fire by night to make their way to success across the Jordan. There is no such thing as "borrowed" vision.

You must have your own dream, your own vision, and measurable goals to tug you on; no one else's will do. Not even God's encouragement persuades those who do not own a personal vision of future success.

If there is anything the Exodus story demonstrates, it is *Lesson Five:* You cannot make someone be a success, or do anything he does not believe in.

Most people do not believe in success—for themselves, anyway. I say most, meaning that nominal 95 percent again. If they believed, they would try. That is why this book is not for everybody. I knowingly devote my words and time to the success-seeking positive 5 percent that tries—a population half the size of Canada. Five Percenters need less urging to set goals and are eager to learn from anyone who offers them help in seeking honest success.

If 5 percent seems a discouragingly small audience, it is not. Only 5 percent of the population bought one of the most famous books of recent history—Norman Vincent Peale's *The Power of Positive Thinking*.

That turned out to be a huge fifteen million copies, but represents only 5 percent of all the people who have been alive in the United States—three hundred million—since the book first saw print in 1952. Five percent is enough to make a difference.

I'm content to labor among the vital 5 percent, the goal-driven few who produce the otherwise-missing half of the world's abundance. Who talks to these world-changers? The mass media ignore this creative minority to feed daily mind-mush to millions, for that is where they make money. Little or nothing is written, said, or done to help this handful who make abundance possible for the rest of society.

Five Percenters are bold souls who change our world by standing on the edge of the future, pulling us along toward their goals, leaving this world better than they found it. If you are among this number, it is because you have chosen to be. It is not a matter of birth or right or anything outside of you. It is your own inner decision that leads you to try making something more of God's world. In so doing, you enter into God's work.

It was while serving as Dr. Peale's personal consultant and fund-raising writer for eighteen years, traveling a total half-million miles to spend two days a month with him, his wife, and staff, that I learned how few people really believe enough in success (as I then understood it) even to try.

I wrote Peale's outgoing mailings and had access to his incoming mail. These millions of letters were regularly summarized and categorized and prayed over, if requested. From the mail I saw, most people profess very humble goals—if you consider as goals things they ask outsiders to pray for.

Such ordinary things! A peaceful home life. Someone to love. Children who would love back. Companionship. A healed body. A healed relationship. A new start. Solace over loss. Enough to make do with, but rarely a call for abundance, and never, never a prayer for riches.

For some time this lack of high-targeting concerned me. Most of it, money could not buy. Yet from access to the Peale ministry and world leaders in his circle, I knew the fantastic power of a goal well-chosen, the reality of success properly envisioned, the creativity of minds and hearts joined in prayer, and the certainty of unexpected help in the darkest hour for those who believed.

What could not these seekers after Peale's prayers have and do, I thought, if they but gave themselves permission to set goals that were higher (in my opinion)!

I understood success then, as others do, only in the business sense, forgetting the homey, homely kind God promised His people upon leaving Egypt. The kind of success where every man dwells under his own vine and fig tree and feels himself blessed to live long enough to see his grandchildren—that's the Old Testament ideal.

At its peak of national power and wealth under Solomon, the writer of 1 Kings 4:25 can find no greater way to describe the nation's happy state than to say, "As long as he lived, the people throughout Judah and Israel lived in safety, each family with its own grapevines and fig trees."

Here we see the Bible's model family, successful in supporting itself, its prosperity made possible by wise political leadership that maintained the long peace that kept the people safe.

SUCCESS IN TWO POWERS

Success, it becomes clear after long reflection on the Bible and the world it challenges, is of two kinds. Success comes in two "powers," a first and a second, each for a different arena, both for the same ultimate purpose:

Success[1] —Business or career success outside home.
Success[2] —Family success at home—the most important one and God's reason for the other kind.

This common purpose explains why all success goals must be life-enhancing. They must benefit the greatest life-enhancing institution on earth: the family.

- The continuance of human life on earth is God's reason for the family.
- Success helps families survive and prosper.

This is not to say anyone denied family is denied all success. Mother Teresa, who saw in every sufferer a member of God's family in need of help, did not fail in her work, though her solemn vows allowed her no family of her own.

PRIME SUCCESS IS ALL BUSINESS

Success[1] ("Prime Success") spans all business, professional, and career achievement.

Prime Success—what we ordinarily mean by success—is the engine of industry. It empowers the goal-driven few to follow their inner vision, not conform to the common blindness. Prime Success generates the vital surplus that makes a society rich enough to support the less capable and give a good life to all who will work for it.

Though widely sought, it is attained by only a few, as we have seen, perhaps as few as 5 percent. Pre-industrial cultures discouraged this kind of success outright. They feared it led to competition, which, in small, closed groups can be destructive. Tribal peoples and self-satisfied groups still pressure their fellows to lower or forsake personal success goals for the sake of unity.

Prime Success, *i.e.*, success in one's work, expresses itself in physical things and a concern for the future. Being so conspicuous, this is success as the world thinks of it. It's what Five Percenters set out to do.

While generating up to half of all human wealth and 100 percent of our greatest advances, Prime Success does not automatically bring us happiness. That is not its purpose! The purpose of work-success is to provide abundance to forestall disaster, so the human race can prosper.

SUCCESS TO A HIGHER POWER

Success[2] ("Family Success") is, by contrast, given for the sake of our happiness, not to make wealth.

Unlike its business cousin, this brand of success is not limited to a minority of high-achieving adults. Home-focused, not work-based, it is meant for all people who dwell on Earth in peace with love.

If "getting what you hope for" is success, then family success is the main source of human joy. Most of our hopes center on our homes. Family Success bases itself on the ordinary things of life, not the extraordinary. It's the very opposite of career-success, where the idea is to achieve the unusual!

And as I saw in Dr. Peale's mailbag, this is the success most people have in mind when asking others to pray for them. We can never pray as hard for stocks and bonds as we can for the flesh and blood we love.

Family Success—the Bible's ideal of happiness in the home—is found in routines of ordinary life devoted to kin and kindness, friends and posterity. Like happiness and love, and unlike the other success, it cannot be measured.

SUCCESS SUMMARY

✦ Our successes may not endear us to others.
✦ We tend to become what we inwardly see ourselves being.
✦ It is not reality that halts success so much as our giant fears.
✦ No one can be forced to be successful.
✦ Prime Success is expressed in careers.
✦ Family Success is the source of most happiness.

Scripture references
[1] Numbers 13:33
[2] Numbers 11:5

Worry is really
a negative prayer

—*prayer in reverse*—

that can bring upon us
exactly what we
do *not* want
and fear the most.

Success and Master Mind Groups

Look at the crows:
they don't plant seeds or gather a harvest;
they don't have storage rooms or barns;
God feeds them!
You are worth so much more than birds!
Can any of you live a bit longer
by worrying about it?
Luke 12:24–25

*I*n the Bible, success takes two forms: Success in living and success in achieving; that is, family success and work success, or success in the home and outside the home.

Knowing this, it becomes easier to deal with some of the "hard sayings" of Jesus like the one quoted above. Here, as Jesus chain-linked parables into a sermon for a crowd of thousands, He had in mind Success-to-the-Higher-Power, home success. It supplies our "daily bread" as we trust in God and focus on grateful prayer, not on worry.

Worry is negative prayer or prayer-in-reverse that can bring us exactly what we do *not* want by making it the focus of our thought-life and inadvertent actions. We tend to get, to do, or to fall into what we

147

think about most. This makes mind-filling prayer the better option in times of trouble.

Assurance of God's concern for our daily bread is a comfort to all believers, but *success-seekers hear in it a second message,* one of permission to achieve other goals, believing God will provide the basics. The promise frees them to focus more on their goals, less on daily concerns for which God has already committed Himself.

Trusting God for the necessaries lets them shift focus from short-term to long-term goals, to activities that improve the future instead of patching up the past. In the end, God says He will provide. That promise opens up the future.

We must recognize the economic conditions in which Jesus spoke and in which His words were repeated for the next one thousand seven hundred years. Like the people, times were universally poor, remaining that way for almost everyone until the American and Industrial Revolutions.

History repeated itself each generation. Always, a few had much, the many had little. Since moving into cities, mankind knew no other way. Poverty was a universal condition of the race, in part because social structures were so primitive.

We marvel at the magnificent works of engineering, art, and governance of the Greco-Roman period in which Jesus ministered. Yet their institutions in producing wealth or transmitting it to other times and places lagged.

Even the Caesars, all-powerful as some were, were limited by this lag. If one wanted to designate a political successor, the only effective way, given the state of law at the time, was to adopt the successor—perhaps his junior by only a few years—as his heir. Then the office could be passed on. Other methods, such as wills and senate resolutions, were unreliable and subject to corruption.

Then something happened that took humanity from universal poverty to increasingly universal opportunity.

SUCCESS-SEEKER CLASS BORN

You have only to look at a graph of world population from Roman times until now to sense that something happened around two hundred years ago. Whatever it was, it changed everybody's opportunities from there on. For the population "curve," which had been prairie-flat for hundreds of years, started sloping through foothills of growth and today is at Mount Everest peaks.

That "something" was new attitudes and ideas—and the birth of the success-seeking Five Percent Class with the Industrial Revolution.

Until the Industrial Revolution, individual boldness and daring were quenched wherever they appeared, except on the battlefield. As a threat to the easy life of the inherited-power class, bold success-seekers were always picked off, one by one, as they surfaced, until the Industrial Revolution shifted the source of wealth from land owners and put it in the hands of entrepreneurs.

When society changed during the Renaissance, it had grown rich exploiting the rediscovered "old knowledge" of the ancient Greeks. After the Industrial Revolution began, society grew even richer, faster, exploiting the new knowledge born of free inquiry. This new knowledge fostered individual action. It created novel situations where wealth could rapidly be gained by bold and imaginative individual acts. It was individual action, collectively, that opened North America to rapid European settlement.

It shows in our family trees. On my mother's side I descend from Finns who came to America singly; one to escape the czar's army, others to work in the timber or the new iron mines of upper Michigan a century ago.

My grandfather on my father's side was an army scout who served in the West after the Civil War. His aunt and uncle raised him after the death of his parents when he was a boy. His grandfather before him had been orphaned, too—his parents killed by Indians, I am told, soon after his birth. In my grandmother's family (the source of my Native American blood), there was a Hessian mercenary who stayed behind in America after the Revolution, using his mustering-out pay from King George to begin a new life. But everyone we trace in our clan made a personal, individual choice to come to this continent. Many readers would find the same to be true for them.

Individual choices, actions, and investments laid the foundation for the America we know today. This individualistic heritage—which finds support in the Bible stories of David, Samson, Moses, and Elijah—shows in our Daniel Boone tales, our legends of Johnny Appleseed, stories about the solitude of Abraham Lincoln, and pictures of George Washington kneeling in prayer at Valley Forge.

SUCCESS NO SOLO ACT

Individualism is our legend. It is also our downfall. For if things go wrong, and success becomes failure, that too is our personal responsibility. Or so we tell ourselves. It is a mistake to imagine success is *our* achievement alone.

We need to see success and failure (temporary non-success) in their full light—as something more than one-person victories or setbacks.

Among the great writers on success was Napoleon Hill, who flourished from the turn of the twentieth century until the 1960s. His most remembered works, based on years of interviews with the richest and most successful persons of the period, came out in the 1930s. In particular, his book *Think and Grow Rich*[1] had a life-changing impact on thousands, including me.

Second only to the Bible, this book changed my life. Hill is credited with creating more millionaires than anyone in history by isolating and teaching the principles of success. His books continue to sell long after his death.

Hill's lifelong study of the success-patterns of America's great achievers revealed something unexpected. Contrary to common belief, *the successful rarely succeeded totally on their own*. Others helped them on the way. He generalized his observations into some loose rules:

THE RULES FOR RICHES

- No one gets rich slowly. Wealth typically comes fast or not at all.
- No one gets rich alone. Others get rich with you, and help you get rich.
- So form a "master mind" group of allies to speed the flow of vital ideas, contacts, and answers to reach your shared goals.

True, the giants of success Hill quizzed, powerful individuals who bestrode the growing industrial colossus of America from the early 1900s through World War II, took decisive individual actions. Yet all were aided by a "third mind" in the collective brainpower of a "master mind" group dedicated to their success.

Over the years I've been part of potent "master mind" groups. One to which I belonged—and still attend when I can—meets monthly at a hilltop ranch in the Texas hill country. Men and women, about 20 in all, come from as far as Oklahoma City, Dallas, Houston, Nashville, and Mexico. Some fly by corporate jet to a small airport nearby. Others get picked up at San Antonio, 100 miles south. I usually come the farthest when I attend.

They gather monthly in the glass-walled quarter-acre parlor of entrepreneur Walter Hailey,[2] one of the remarkable sales success teachers of our time. Gazing upon the transparently green Guadalupe River below, where dinosaur footprints under water look like they were made in yesterday's mud, one imagines a long-necked brontosaurus could peer into the meeting any time. In this room, anything seems possible.

These committed, capable people gather to reach shared goals and to offer each other their best ideas, contacts, and judgments to that end. They share wisdom and insights to be found nowhere but in this trusted circle.

In the end more than enrichment is involved, for new risk-taking ventures get born here. If successful, these result in new jobs that feed the babies of unknown families in distant places. Few people would believe how much new wealth is created for everyone by such Master Mind groups as this.

Hailey, who says that Jesus and His disciples were the first Master Mind group, defines the Master Mind as

> *Two or more minds joined together*
> *in perfect harmony*
> *toward a major purpose, goal,*
> *or magnificent obsession.*

"These minds together create a 'master mind' which is greater than the sum of the parts," he says. "Now 'one and one' can add up to a billion."

Unhampered by negative thinkers, the doubtful, and the unfocused, a functioning Master Mind is an engine for achievements that might otherwise take lifetimes.

POWER FOR CRYING OUT LOUD

It took me awhile to see that in all my years of charity work with Norman Vincent Peale we operated intuitively as a kind of Master Mind Success Group. We met monthly with the stated purpose of finding new ways to bless people with the gospel. It was after one such meeting I went home and conceptualized in detail what became Dr. Peale's world-famous *Positive Thinkers Club*, an institution now widely copied.

A Master Mind demands perfect harmony, nothing less. Working with charities and businesses over the years, I've sometimes asked for the removal of some negative person from our meeting.

When creative thinking is needed, ill-spirited people must leave. Otherwise, nothing worthwhile can happen. Some people emanate hate-waves, negativity, and disruptive feelings that can be picked up on radar. No Master Mind Group can function in the midst of bad attitudes. Those who cannot be positive must leave the room—or wear lead shielding, I say.

Jesus spoke of "two or three" coming together in His name to obtain from God what they need. He also said, "Whenever two of you on earth agree about anything you pray for, it will be done for you . . ." [3] There is a peculiar thing, however, about the form of this mutual agreement. The word used here in the Bible for "agree" means "to sound or speak together."

The Bible seems to say that a goal mutually desired must be agreed-to aloud, jointly, in spoken words, not, it seems, in silence; perhaps not even in writing.

(Ask your favorite neighborhood theologian about this. I'm just pointing out what the Bible says. Seven other words in Scripture get translated *agree*, but speak-aloud agreement is the meaning Saint Matthew chose to report what Jesus said. It must mean something.)

I've taken this literally, only because it's there in the Bible. Yet this speak-aloud principle seems universal. It may be why groups that seek specific goals (armies, sports teams, sales groups, Japanese workers) recite their aims in unison. Hailey's sales seminars follow this rule, roaring frequent affirmations of goal and purpose, chanted loudly by the group many times in a four-day training session.

I advocate that believers, if planning a Master Mind Group to achieve some worthy goal, see themselves as a *Master's* Mind Success group. The difference is subtle yet significant.

Hailey points out that Jesus worked no miracles, according to the Bible's own account, before forming the first Master Mind Group, His chosen disciples, who sought to know and do the Master's will.

The power of joined minds around a shared, spoken, single-minded goal is so strong it sometimes seems an "extra mind" is in operation, a super-brain greater than the sum of the parts present.

This extra dimension has nothing to do with brainstorming. Nor is it demonism. It is the true Master Mind and one of the secrets behind great success in business.

This power is not available to those who treat success as a one-man show. The lone hunter, the lone plainsman, the lone inventor, the lone leader never were as alone in their successes as legend would have it. There is still One other in whom we live and move and have our being—and find our successes.

We who choose to be of the super-productive Five Percenters need to be single-hearted, but we can never do our best work singly. We need the collective excitement, encouragement, and wisdom of minds other than our own, agreeing with us in our purposes and prayers, if we are to reach our highest goals on earth.

We need the power of the Master's mind as well, if it is true success we seek.

Success Summary

✦ Worry is prayer-in-reverse that can bring on the evil we fear too well.
✦ Individual success is not an individual achievement.
✦ Success is easier and more likely to be achieved with the help of a Master Mind success group.
✦ When two or three gather in Jesus' name to ask for God's help, their agreement in prayer, ideally, needs to be "speak-aloud agreement."

Footnotes and Scripture references

[1] Hill, Napoleon. *Think and Grow Rich.* (New York: Fawcett, 1987).

[2] Planned Marketing Associates, Box 345, Hunt, TX 78024

[3] Matthew 18:19

Frugality is
man's way
of sharing
poverty.

Success is
God's way
of sharing
abundance.

Success for You and Yours—On Earth As It Is in Heaven

The LORD says:
. . . I alone know the plans I have for you,
plans to bring you prosperity
and not disaster,
plans to bring about
the future you hope for.
Jeremiah 29:10–11

"*To* bring about the future you hope for" is the Bible's simple phrase for success.

In the Latin roots of the word *prosperity*—"to get what you hope for"—we earlier found the same concept. God is not against success. The Bible shows quite the opposite.

God concerns Himself for the prosperity of His people, going so far as to make plans for it that we don't even know about, as Jeremiah says. Amazing to think He has plans for our success before we do. Where we have hopes, He already has plans!

ASKING FOR TOO LITTLE

Those able to hope for much, who only ask for a little—and get it—*are they successful?* Or are they "unprofitable servants" of the kind the Bible condemns?

They get only what they hope for, not all God planned for, and that I suppose is punishment enough. But we have to ask, *Is it wise to aim below God's best plans for us?*

We are not obligated to get rich. Or to be poor.

But if we shun success without trying, we should shun the parables of Jesus as well. For in them the profit theme echoes loudly, the theme of servants displeasing a master by failing to make full and profitable use of a resource put in their hand.[1]

All success concerns the productive use of material possessions. This is also the theme underlying most of Jesus' parables. Christ's most frequent topic was our making the right use of what God gives us.

THE OPPOSITE OF SUCCESS IS NOT FAILURE

In one of the Weeping Prophet's few happy verses, quoted at the start of this chapter, stands an important clue to God's purpose in wanting us to succeed. It's revealed by two words not usually found together and put there in dramatic opposition. We learn that the antithesis of prosperity (success) is not a genteel non-prosperity, or downright poverty, nor even failure.

The opposite of success is disaster.

Disaster and success, life's two balancing extremes, emboss the two sides of the coin of survival. Those who say they "live on the edge," may not know how aptly they speak. Survival is a coin-on-edge balancing act between nothing and plenty.

Success brings the plentitude that assures survival, a fact our abundant times make us lose sight of. Even when success is commonplace, it is always the fruit of a tiny 5 percent minority who turn "almost-enough" into plenty for all.

- Success is not poverty in reverse gear.
- Success is not an unfair favoring of a few greedy souls at others' expense.
- Success is God's offsetting abundance to replace past and future loss.

Prosperity balances disaster. It restores "the years that the locust hath eaten."[2] It supplies seed-corn and substance to survive future devastation and to build anew. As Joseph in Egypt had the vision to see, success today can be God's hedge against disaster tomorrow, assuring survival for His people until better times return.

> *The most successful is*
> *not the man with the most toys,*
> *but the one who survives hard times*
> *and builds again.*

Without periods of compensating prosperity and success, humanity cannot survive disastrous times. Anyone who seriously reads the Bible knows times of disaster always return and shall become increasingly frequent as the world prepares for the return of Christ.[3]

God has His reasons for success. It's time more Christians respected that.

For seventeen or more centuries it really didn't matter if the mass of Christians entertained fallacious notions of what the Bible said about money, abundance, and prosperity. There never was enough going around to argue over anyway, not until the Industrial Revolution arrived.

During the ninety thousand Lord's Days between Pentecost and the rise of our mechanical civilization, the only thing Believers had in abundance to share was poverty. To be a Christian was to be poor. Everyone was poor.

A few controlled the visible wealth obtained either by inheritance or force. Since the owners usually professed the same religious belief as the workers, the system seemed God-approved: poor on the bottom, rich on the top, with no hope, need, or expectation of any change.

Sermons favoring personal success were unknown. One's local lordling or village squire construed your success as infringing his privileges. (At the time, these ran to such details as demanding you bake your bread in his ovens, for a fee.) Modern notions of personally-earned success were inconceivable. Once success started popping up, it was denounced as sin, as no kinder logic existed to explain the sudden surplus it produced. The devil's work for sure! Success was labeled greed out of control.

To lust for a million ducats in a medieval dukedom worth only a million might well be greedy, selfish, covetous, and anything else bad you want to call it. But to quest for a million dollars in a society where new millions are created every week, and earn it by offering a worthwhile product or service to an eager market, is more commendable than covetous. It makes new wealth for everyone.

SHARING POVERTY IS NOT SUCCESS

I believe the Bible. But I do not believe the old sermon notes (still preached from every Sunday somewhere) that made sense only in a steady-state, poverty-based rural society that no longer exists. I hear few sermons telling how to live in the real-time culture that surrounds us, when it comes to Christians and success or money. A few good pulpits make the point. More advocate frugality and the saving of money, though saving money never made anyone rich except a banker.

- Frugality is humanity's way of sharing poverty.
- Success is God's way of sharing abundance.

Frugality suppresses need in the name of poverty or a greater good. Praiseworthy to be sure, frugality is no substitute for limitless abundance from good success.

The problems of this planet, from hunger upward, can be ameliorated by frugality. But only fresh, abundant resources unleased by success-seekers can ever supply the physical means for resolving them.

Our churches know too little about money. Ministers are taught to fear it, as I've found when speaking in seminaries about fund-raising. The topic offends many student pastors. They laugh, then get angry. God calls them to higher things.

Money-wary professors teach them to avoid lucre as a spiritual contaminant. The net effect is to convince the clergy it's God's will they stay underpaid. They make money unimportant and themselves irrelevant to our culture.

Still, the believer's money is holy money. It is our crystallized sweat, our life and work, stored up in a form to be delivered and used anywhere, for good or evil. We Christians must plan to leverage its use, or others less godly will. Once our labor has been transmuted into money, we cannot disclaim responsibility for how its power gets used. Otherwise, like our taxes, it can be used against what we believe in.

Some misread Scripture and drop three critical words from Paul's comment,[4] thereby making a lie of it. It is *the love of money* that is the root of all evil. Such a misreading is no excuse for the rest of us to fear money or success.

Jesus never said that any physical thing is evil. Money itself cannot be evil anymore than a knife, a cup, or a flame can be—though all can be used wrongly.

If the *love* of money is the root of all evil, then *hatred* of it, I suggest, is the leaf and stem. The fruit of money-hatred is to deny success wholesale to Christians, knocking out of the success business the best people on God's earth to handle it.

Money, the universal communicator, affects everything we do or touch in a complex society such as ours. *This* is the civilization we're living in—not the expired cultures of never-enough in which mankind dwelt till recently, to which most money-sermons still preach. *This* is the only civilization we can witness the gospel's power to. The others are dead and gone. We can't sit this one out.

Ours is a money culture. Disliking it won't change it. We must talk the common language, or society will neither hear nor respect our Christian witness, for we shall seem to speak an unknown tongue, the like of Coptic or Old Slavonic, dead church languages of the past. If money talks, make it speak in Christian terms!

We can't throw up our hands—with money in them—and disclaim responsibility for what it can do. We have to reclaim our long-held belief, misplaced early in this century of war when nations started to seem more important than the people in them, that

1) Personal success is a desirable goal under God.
2) Some beneficial human progress is possible even in corrupt times.
3) Honest money can be used as a tool to serve godly goals.

Until the Lord returns, we have the duty to remain faithful—which means to persist in doing what is right: witnessing, working, and succeeding, if that is His plan for us. The game isn't over till the fat angel sings.

GIVING GOD A BAD REPUTATION

In framing an updated Bible theology of success, *the first problem* is the false notion that money itself (and therefore success) is evil. This holds back many good people from prosperity they have every right to earn.

The second problem is that millions think of success like divine healing, unavailable to ordinary people except by a special miracle. They do not know it is a natural process that responds to work and trust in God. So they overlook the simple rules for success while searching for outlandish "miracle money" schemes that do not exist, and get scammed in return.

The third problem is a bizarre new belief that we can get God to make us rich if we send Him bribes by mail. This widespread odd teaching was fostered by a fringe of radical revivalists who purchased vast amounts of media exposure to teach a dubious doctrine that—whatever it did for others—made them quickly rich.

Building on a beautiful verse[5] in the last book of the Old Testament where the prophet gives God's promise of bumper crops to Jewish farmers of his day in return for delivery of 10 percent of their produce to the temple warehouse, mail-order sects persuaded thousands to mail them millions every month. With torqued tongue they asserted: *"Send US your money and that will prove to God you trust Him, so He can entrust you with even more!"*

Of hundreds of media ministries in America, most are small and struggle to pay their bills and keep their gospel witness alive. (For years I've taught seminars on how to raise the funds they need, honestly.) But just as bad money drives out good, a few—the 5 percent rule again—gained a large following for a novel "get God, get rich" scheme among the generation born since lotteries became legal.

Today many of the working poor practice this TV-taught lottery religion, tipping God in hope of a big win, like buying a lottery ticket. Payouts are determined not by a computer or a random drawing, but by obscure readings from the Bible. The way to God's ear is paying, not praying.

Teachings like this give God a bad reputation among the unknowing. The cash flow from this warped doctrine is wasted on high overhead, high living, and useless projects having little to do with the gospel. (As a fund-raiser, I see such wasteful abuses in sharper detail than most.)

Such media-born heresy makes its mark because more orthodox Christian thinkers retain out-of-date ideas about money and success. They teach the young and new converts that success is the first step to turning away from God. So we abandon the field to the exploiters. We fail to see success as the tool of God it has always been—*the Gleeful Grower that offsets the Grim Reaper.*

THE LAST OF THE CHRISTIANS

Our churches shall become quaint religious fossils—like some of the Amish sects and the few surviving Shakers—if we do not update our thinking about success to fit today's world and the nonagrarian times we live in.

If we shun "worldly" success in favor of suntanning the soul in private, we will have no place in our own land. Without successful men and women in our ranks to create wealth for our people and times, God's people shall be without power and without respect from those who govern. Color Christianity as good as gone, for all the influence or safety we'll have.

God may indeed have plans for our success, as Jeremiah says, but it is perfectly possible to aim below what He intends. *No law says another full generation of misled, success-scorning Christians can't end up as America's low-paid "hewers of wood," "drawers of water," and servers of burgers.*

If we refuse to let some of us learn to get rich, we will all be poor, defeating God's plans for our prosperity and denying Christians any cultural leadership in the future.

Personal business success must again become respectable among Christians. It may involve only 5 percent of us, at best, but stands to benefit everyone. Success-hating will have to go the way of carping preachments once heard against telephones, motor cars, and women voting, for it is just as relevant. We can worship our past or change the future, but not both.

Three attitudes must change. None of them has a thing to do with the Bible, only with false notions some church people retain, rooted in peasant fatalism.

We must quit teaching our young that it's wrong to burn, to learn, and to earn.

- Quit telling them it's wrong to burn with desire to achieve something good for man—which can be measured with numbers—as well as something great for God, which cannot be judged until heaven. There can be no success of any kind without strong, burning desire to achieve something good on earth. Let God sort it out. His glory is not enhanced by our squelching of God-given talents.
- Quit telling them it's wrong to learn more because they'll get puffed up with knowledge or the devil will mislead them. All we do now by keeping them from superior education is assure that the fewest Christians get the really good jobs, the cutting-edge jobs that pay the most and offer a leading role in changing a society that is clearly headed for hell without them.
- Quit telling them, subtly, it's wrong to earn more because riches are a temptation to sin. (Poverty is more of a temptation.) We sanctify poverty because Jesus lived poor among us, but He left other examples we choose not to follow. Besides being poor, Jesus never married, had no family or home of His own, and died in His

169

thirties. Is that what we want for our children? The life of Christ and the Christian life are not identical.

When we look at the subject closely, it is clear many things widely believed about Christian success are virtual superstition, never held up to the mirror or seen in any light except the devil's torch of self-consuming envy.

We've got to quit saying negative things about godly success-seekers that we cannot, upon examination, seriously defend! The consequences are too great.

We, too, can disappear!

One of the first strongholds of Christianity was North Africa. For six productive centuries the church there grew, taught, and evangelized. Then it vanished forever with barely a ripple, swallowed in the rising sea of early Islam.

Just as Christianity disappeared overnight from North Africa in the seventh century, and communism from Russia in the twentieth, Christianity can disappear from North America in the twenty-first. That is, if Christians persist in acting on self-destructive, non-biblical notions whose effects impoverish us as a people and rob us of influence in our country.

A deliberate lack of success is no proof of God's favor.

If Bible believers continue to refuse the burden of success, Christians shall enjoy a smaller and smaller say in the America they built. The Bible's moral bulwarks, the very foundations of the American way of life and system of government, will get swept away by waves of homegrown barbarians and energetic aliens from other cultures not afraid of success.

Why are Christians today so afraid of success? What have we got to lose? Our souls? Hardly! Our reputations? *What* reputations? Public respect? *What* respect? We get less of that every passing day.

All we have left to lose is—our beloved country.

The land of the free and the home of the brave may be home to us no more. The Christian faith will be part of America's past, not its future.

I don't like the prospect. And it does not have to be.

Is it possible success-shunning, by cutting off the power source of America's Bible-based cultural leadership, has something to do with the ghastly moral decline of our time? I fear it does.

LAST CALL FOR AMERICA

This book is a call for a new generation of God's silent success-seekers to rise up and seek openly the prosperity God plans for His people, as shown in the Bible.

You are the minority whose prosperity can create new wealth and political power to protect the godly in their quiet lives. Don't let others hold you back, saying success is unimportant or not a respectable goal for God-fearing people. The Bible shows otherwise.

Your prosperity can bless the rest of God's people, giving us moral power again to lead our nation with more than words, allowing all of

171

us to witness and do all the good we can, for all the people we can, for as long as we can.

Get started. Stand on your major life purpose. Set up your goals. Include God in your plans. Go to work and share your success with everyone you can.

We'll be praying for you. God knows how we need you!

Scripture References
[1] Luke 15–16; Matthew 25
[2] Joel 2:25, KJV
[3] Romans 3:22
[4] 1 Timothy 6:10, KJV
[5] Malachi 3:10

Success by Faith

But those who trust in the LORD for help . . .
will rise on wings like eagles.
Isaiah 40:31

*A*mericans donate generously to find cures but will give little or nothing for prevention.

This discovery proved the most troubling challenge of my years raising funds for God's people and America's great causes. It's easier to get people to give to fight AIDS than to get them to change their behavior to avoid it.

As children of our times, folks want to do what they want to do, yet hope to claim rewards like those who do the right things at the right times. They want to lose weight without dieting, get rich without investment, succeed without effort.

Many books offer them what they want—easy, magic cures. Not this one, for the Bible does not offer them. It offers instead encouragement, examples, and permission.

I write for those who are, or want to be, part of the 5 percent solution, not those who want to kid themselves. So I will not lie to you about success. There is no easy little pill that, swallowed, cures poverty or failure. *Success is a system for getting better results from your work than most people get.* Work is what it's all about. The Bible says we have to work. It doesn't say we have to succeed. Yet we have the right to try. This is a book for those who try.

Unlike the Godfather of fiction, the God of all reality makes offers we can refuse. Salvation is one of them. Success in our work, another.

It is not necessarily God's will that we succeed, but it's allowed for in His plans for us, as we saw. We can turn Him down, losing opportunities and rewards, but not our souls. Perhaps our awards in heaven are less if we shun God's plans for our success, I cannot say.

All our work, whether others deem it success or failure, God will one day test by fire. That which survives, if founded on Jesus Christ, will endure to be recognized and rewarded by God. For those who do not believe, the Bible is clear, success cannot buy them heaven.

The Bible bears surprising testimony to God's interest in our success. In Jesus' parable of the good Samaritan (Luke 10) the accepted surprise is *who* God says is our neighbor. It is not just the borrower next door who is deserving of neighborly concern, but also the stranger mugged in the street, direly in need, unable to repay our kindness. (*Mercy* is what you call kindness that cannot be repaid.)

Our *neigh*bor (who "dwells *nigh*" or nearby) is no longer defined by property lines, but by how we use our property in line with God's desire that we show mercy to those in life-or-death need. We can accept *that* surprise.

The true surprise to seekers after God's plan for successful living is the Samaritan's business success, which Jesus simply accepts. That's not really what modern readers expect, given the common belief that the Bible hates the well-off. From millions of examples Jesus might have chosen, He took a successful businessman, from an unpopular social minority at that. Then He said of this unlikely model, *"Go, and do thou likewise."* Imitate that person! We sense more here to imitate than an act of unplanned mercy.

To Jesus' audience, being Samaritan was a spittable offense. They were despised racially and religiously. Any success such outcasts enjoyed clearly did not come of God's special blessing but by following natural laws available to anyone—even a disadvantaged Samaritan.

The so-called good Samaritan did not belong to the idle rich. He worked hard for a good living, spending nights on the road away from his family, pursuing his business. No staff helped him to and from Jericho. He owned a modest means of transportation, had money in his purse, and good credit besides. He sounds more the American business success than anyone else in the Bible.

The Samaritan Success had the wrong religion, wrong race, wrong education, but the right goals, right methods, and right attitudes for business success. *He used success the way God intended, sharing it, helping someone whose urgent need others ignored. For this Jesus commended him— and him to us.*

SECRETS? WHAT SECRETS?

Why are the basic laws of success always considered "secrets"? If Samaritans, Babylonians, Greeks, Phoenicians, and modern Britons, Americans, and others have constantly rediscovered them, why are they still deemed hidden knowledge, secrets not plainly open to everyone?

It depends on who's talking.

To the goal-directed, success-driven 5 percent, it's no secret, just practical wisdom to be sought out, studied, and applied to one's life. Since the dawn of history, the other 95 percent miss the point. It's betrayed by the hidden scorn in the word they invented to describe their ever-richer neighbors' puzzling behavior: "Business = busy + ness = Lively but meaningless activity."

Not understanding how one man's goals can change everyman's future, the 95 percent like to think business is really trivial busy-ness, a ritual rain dance to inattentive gods of fortune. They see little link between lively activity today and success tomorrow. They fail to attribute a power to goals. Five Percenters don't make that mistake.

PERMISSION GRANTED

The truly secret—or unnoticed—difference between success-seekers and all others starts at the point of Permission. Here, from Chapter 1, are listed the four generally known steps to success, excluding Permission, which only the fortunate few know is the turnstile barring entry to a better future for most people.

1) Set a measurable goal.
2) Hold a clear vision of that goal.
3) Form a plan to reach the goal.
4) Follow your plan to reach the goal.

None of this is new unless you are hearing it for the first time. Chopped, minced, spiced up, blended, adulterated, or mixed with air, it's a program found in every success tract ever published. And it works if you come prepared.

You find rules like this on Sumerian clay and Egyptian papyrus, and their echoes in the Bible. The principles of success-building are no different from building a pyramid in Pharaonic times or a house in our own.

1) You decide to build the house of your dreams.
2) You pre-visualize its size, shape, site, and cost.
3) You buy plans or hire an architect to draw them.
4) Your contractor follows the plans step-by-step.

For most people, for most of history, this has been enough. You dreamed, you planned, you worked, hoping for success. Life was short, opportunities rare. Only after the positive effects of the Industrial Revolution began to be felt, giving more people more years, more health, and more hopes, did the four-step model of success start failing. Not that it did not go far enough. *It does not start soon enough.*

What's missing, we see in our new understanding of success—listed in Chapter 6 and summarized here—the secular phrase on the left, its Bible equivalent on the right:

0) Firm Desire . . . . One's Major Life Purpose
1) Permission . . . . Finding authority for success
2) Goal-Setting . . . . Inspiring vision of future desired
3) Goal-Picturing . . . . Repeat imaging of success in prayer
4) Goal-Striving . . . . Working toward success
5) Goal Reached . . . . Success *(Thank you, Lord!)*

Our new model sees success as a six-level, five-step staircase. It recognizes that success does not start with Goal-Setting, but two steps earlier, with assertion of one's underlying Major Life Purpose. *Success is whatever fulfills that purpose.*

Those grounded in the Bible know pretty well what their Major Life Purpose is. It's something "inborn-again," a spliced-in godliness gene prepackaged with their new spiritual nature. Others pick up Purpose from families or early life experiences.

However said, a believer's Major Life Purpose generally has to do with pleasing God and helping others. Such clear Purpose gives distinct advantages. It frees believers to deal with the next step, our deep, unspoken human need for Permission—permission to run the risk of success.

If faith means trusting God,
Permission means trusting ourselves
at the same time.

Permission is an eaglet peering over the nest rim one last time, casting off timidity, ready at last to trust God's invisibly solid air and his own untried wings to sustain a soaring new life, one to be lived ever after between heaven and earth.

Those who trust in the LORD for help . . .
will rise on wings like eagles.

$\mathcal{M}$y First Steps to Career $\mathcal{S}$uccess

Knowing the choice is mine, under God, am I ready to pay the price, in hard work and persistence, to strive to be one of the successful 5 percent in my business or career?_____

—FIRM DESIRE—

✔ Have I found my clear Major Life Purpose?_____

✔ If so, what is it? (If you can't say it in ten or twenty words, you need to think about it some more.)_____

_____

_____

—PERMISSION—

✔ Have I Permission to *Succeed* . . .
or only Permission to *Try*?_____

✔ Where did I get my Permission?_____

✔ If I still need Permission, how can I get it?_____

—GOAL SETTING—

☑ Based on my Major Life Purpose, what are my goals?
(Valid goals are measurable, specific, life-enhancing.)
Ask yourself: *What will I give in exchange for what I get, and how will I measure my success?* Lacking numbers, a goal is only a dream or a wish. You must be able to measure success to know when you achieve it and are ready for new goals. How will your goals bless and help others?

_____

_____

_____

_____

_____

Date _____   Signed _____

The Further Steps to Success

—GOAL-PICTURING—

☑ Keep the image of my coming success before myself and before God, seeing it now as a present reality to act upon in faith.

In frequent prayer, visualize yourself as a success, enjoying the substance of things hoped for and reaping the rewards of your work. Do *not*, as many mistakenly do, picture yourself *doing* the work. Focus on the end, not the process. See the result, not the routine, or you may discourage yourself by making the effort seem tiresome.

—GOAL-STRIVING—

☑ As I work at achieving my goals, I shall stay alert for new opportunities disguised as problems.

You may wish to pray for a bigger vision of success, as your goals get tempered with experience and you discover new opportunities. Refer always to your Major Life Purpose. Not every idea is one you should invest in. Use old goals as stepping stones to new ones. Most successful people upgrade their goals as they go along, once they find out how many opportunities open up for them.

—GOAL REACHED!—

 I must have further plans when I reach my success goal, so that I will not undo my work and God's blessing by aimless living.

When humans get bored they do dumb things like messing up their lives, undoing the enterprises that made them prosper, and forgetting God. Then they have to start all over again. To avoid this risk, keep growing, keep adding new goals as old ones are realized, and keep trying to be a blessing to others.

Can I Be Happy As a Success?

The world would like you to think happiness and success are enemies. But happiness is merely a continuing attitude of joyful anticipation, nothing more. If the path to success is filled with anticipation, it is enough to keep many goal-seekers happy.

What most people deeply crave, however, is more akin to contentment—being full of the shared joys of family and friends—found in doing simple things. Since high achievement tends to isolate us, we need to invest time in people and causes we love and root ourselves in the Bible.

"Why Fear Success?"

A Testimony By the Author

𝑀Y LAST BOSS EVER, before I launched my first successful business, was billionaire Arthurs S. DeMoss, whose faith lay in God, not his money. We traveled the land teaching charities to reach high goals. As my mentor, he freely shared his secrets of personal success and taught me an uncomfortable truth:

> *Success follows God-given natural laws*
> *that work alike for sinner and saint.*

He was right. Basic laws of success were old when the pyramids were new. Even bad people can succeed or prosper (*"get what they hope for"*) if they obey the rules. Today these old laws form the core of most books on success. That's why so many sound alike.

HIDDEN PATTERNS

In the fourteen months I took from other work to write this book, I stumbled—or was led—into a pattern of distinctive principles about success *found in the Bible and nowhere else*. Here was a trove the world forgot or never knew—the most complete concept of success I'd ever seen.

In all, *Seven Biblical Laws of Success* stood out. Only two or three are widely known.

As more of these unexpected patterns showed up, my bafflement turned to amazement. Success, as God planned it, clearly was something different from what most Americans think! The whole notion of success in our time is tainted. People wrongly link *success* with *excess*.

That's why many Christians today shun success, though once we freely sought it and used our personal success—with God's help—to trigger the prosperity that made America great.

GOD'S PLAN FOR YOU

God's purpose in success is to create rapid abundance TODAY for us to survive tough times tomorrow. That's all.

Why fear success? Our fear is an American heresy, not a biblical truth. If we can trust God to help us when poor, why can't we trust Him for times of abundance? The Bible shows Him willing to trust You. Why not trust Him back? It's called faith.

Christian Motivational Institute
Box 190 • Glen, New Hampshire 03838
Publishers of the
Success Mentor®Newsletter and
study guides for this book.
Send stamped envelope for free report:
"How to Succeed Like a Christian."